Spirits
of the
Snow

MYTH AND MANKIND

Spirits
of the
Snow

ARCTIC MYTH

MYTH AND MANKIND

SPIRITS OF THE SNOW: Arctic Myth
Writers: Tony Allan (The Peoples of the Far North, Ritual and the Bonds of Community), Charles Phillips (The Soul of the Wild, The Legacy of Arctic Myth), Michael Kerrigan (Shadows of Creation; Tricksters, Culture Heroes and Shamans)
Consultant: Dr Piers Vitebsky

Created, edited and designed by
Duncan Baird Publishers
Castle House
75–76 Wells Street
London W1P 3RE

DUNCAN BAIRD PUBLISHERS
Managing Editor: Diana Loxley
Managing Art Editor: Clare Thorpe
Series Editor: Christopher Westhorp
Editor: Mark McDowall
Designer: Clare Thorpe
Picture Researcher: Cecilia Weston-Baker
Commissioned Illustrations: Neil Gower
Map Artwork: Lorraine Harrison
Artwork Borders: Iona McGlashan
Editorial Researcher: Hannah Bolus

TIME-LIFE BOOKS
Time-Life INC. President and CEO: George Artandi
Time-Life International President: Stephen R. Frary

Staff for SPIRITS OF THE SNOW: Arctic Myth
Editorial Manager: Tony Allan
Design Consultant: Mary Staples
Editorial Production: Ruth Vos

Published by Time-Life Books BV, Amsterdam
First Time-Life English language printing 1999
TIME-LIFE is a trademark of
Time Warner Inc, USA

ISBN 0 7054 3653 5

Colour separation by Colourscan, Singapore
Printed and bound by Milanostampa, SpA, Farigliano, Italy

Title page: **Blue mask symbolizing the spirit of the killer-whale, 20th century. In the killer-whale's mouth is a porpoise and on its back an image of its *inua*, or inner being.**

Contents page: **Carving by Saima Qitsualuk from the Northwest Territories, 20th century. It tells the story of Aqsauyayuq who was challenged by his fellow men for the hand of his beautiful wife.**

30 29 28 27 26 25 24 23 22 21 20 19 18 17 16 15 14 13 12 11 10 9 8 7 6 5 4 3 2

Contents

THE PEOPLES OF THE FAR NORTH

Everything about the far north stretches the imagination, not least its distances: Greenland, as big as western Europe; Canada and Alaska, with almost eight per cent of the world's land area between them; Siberia, stretching a third of the way around the globe and taking in nine time zones on the way.

Then there is the unforgiving weather. One of the coldest places on Earth, Oimyakon, in Siberia, has experienced temperatures as low as minus seventy degrees centigrade; yet in summer the same spot can bask in forty degree heat. In Canada's far north, meteorologists can register winter temperatures below minus twenty degrees centigrade continually for four months at a time.

Yet for all nature's hostility, people have lived in this forbidding land for thousands of years. Life for these frontiersmen has never been easy, and there have never been many of them. Scholars reckon that there were perhaps 60,000 Inuit at the time of European contact in the sixteenth century. And a recent estimate of the total native population of the far north came up with a figure below 600,000. In terms of density per square kilometre, these have always been the loneliest peoples in the world.

But maybe through a sense of that very isolation, northern societies have traditionally been close-knit. They have found little need for any clearly defined political hierarchy, for the virtues of co-operation and sharing have always been paramount in a world in which resources were scarce.

Nature, however, was seen not as hostile but as working by rules which compelled humans to adapt their ways to forces which were far greater than themselves. They had to observe taboos and respect the animals and environment which supported them. For help they could turn to shamans, soul voyagers who journeyed to the spirit world.

In the long winter darkness, it was tales of such quests that kept listeners spellbound as the fire sparked and the Arctic winds whistled outside. For stories also helped in the unremitting struggle for survival: tales that told the terrible consequences of showing disrespect to nature, accounts of shamans' heroic struggles against hostile spiritual forces, or narratives of physical endurance that bore a message of hope in a perilous world.

Opposite: **Koryak people set up camp amid the driving snows of the Kamchatka peninsula in Siberia.**

Below: **An ancient pair of Inuit goggles with built-in protective shade used to prevent blindness caused by the harsh Arctic glare of sun on snow.**

7

The Frozen Lands

Up to the twentieth century, the peoples of the far north had to live off the land. Every aspect of their lives was dedicated to exploiting territories where agriculture was not an option. But for the resourceful, there were abundant rewards to be had amid the Arctic landscape.

The lifestyles the different peoples of the Arctic led were surprisingly similar, being shaped mainly by their access to the region's three geographic zones: taiga, tundra and the coast.

The taiga, as the Russians call their northern forests, takes up a large proportion of the nation's huge landmass, stretching in an almost continuous belt across Siberia from the Ural Mountains to the Pacific Ocean. There are ecologically similar woodlands in Scandinavia and in the high middle latitudes of North America, extending through Canada into Alaska. This is a dark and silent world of mainly coniferous trees – pines, firs, larches and spruces – that in the winter becomes snowbound. This aids, rather than impedes travel, however, for throughout the Arctic people's skill with sledges, skis and snowshoes makes winter transport much easier and faster than in the boggy summer.

The peoples who eked out a living in the sombre forest depths did so mainly by hunting, trapping and fishing. In Siberia, they included the forest Nenets, once known as Samoyed; the Ket, whose tongue is the unique survivor of an otherwise extinct language family; and the Tungus-speaking Even and Evenk, as closely related as their similar names would imply. Their North American equivalents were the most northerly of the Indian peoples, notably the Montagnais, the Tanaina and the Cree.

Much of the forest hunting was of small mammals, but there was one larger creature that bred in vast numbers and that did a great deal to shape the lives of those humans who came into contact with it: *Rangifer tarandus*,

An ice-laden river snakes its way through the snow-covered forests of Yamal in Siberia. This is the land of the Nenets, many of whom still live by herding reindeer.

known in Scandinavia and Siberia as the reindeer and in North America as the caribou.

At first the reindeer was hunted like any other forest quarry, but in Eurasia at some unknown point in prehistory the indigenous peoples learned to herd the beasts. Until very recently, relatively small numbers were involved, for in the forests it was never easy to handle large groups. There the deer were used as much for transport as for food. The herders used them to pull sledges and carry tents and other equipment that would have weighed down human shoulders. In Siberia they learned to ride them like horses.

Things were very different on the forest margins, above the treeline where the taiga gave way to the stunted vegetation of the tundra. To the outsider fly-ing over it in a plane, this vast treeless expanse can look like an empty desert, for little grows here for much of the year. For nine months it is whipped by winter winds that harden the snow into deep drifts. And below the surface is permafrost – permanently frozen ground that in places can be more than a kilometre deep.

Yet in the brief Arctic summer this uncompromising terrain bursts into unexpected life. Above the Arctic Circle, which runs around the Earth at latitude sixty-six degrees north, the sun never sets for at least one day of the year; and beyond latitude seventy-five degrees there is twenty-four-hour sunlight for three whole months. Warmed by its rays, the ice melts back and seeds that have lain dormant through the winter germinate in a thin layer of melted topsoil.

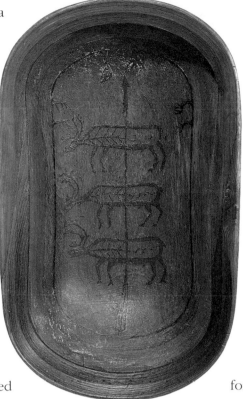

Images of three caribou, surrounded by a thunderbird figure, adorn this wooden Inuit bowl. The revelation of an animal's inner skeleton is related to the vision of the shaman in a trance who can see the hidden nature of animals and people.

The vegetation rapidly attracts other forms of life. Insects swarm over ponds thick with larvae, providing food for millions of migrating wildfowl. Small mammals put in an appearance: Arctic ground squirrels, which hibernate for nine months of the year, lemmings that survive in tunnels beneath the snow. They in turn support larger predators, including Arctic foxes and wolves. But above all the tundra now provides ample fodder for the huge herds of reindeer or caribou, which emerge from their winter refuges in the forests to calve and to browse and grow fat on lichens, sedges and grasses.

And with them go the reindeer herders, accompanying them on a constant nomadic cycle from winter to summer pasturages and back again. This was the lifestyle of the Saami of Scandinavia, once known as the Lapps, as well as the Chukchi, the Koryak and many other Siberian peoples, for whom the deer served as a lifeline in an otherwise inhospitable world.

In North America the situation was different. One of the Arctic's mysteries is that Canada and Alaska never developed a herding culture, even though the caribou there followed the same migratory pattern as the reindeer on the other side of the Bering Strait. The huge herds were exploited but by hunters who would wait for the deer to come to them. They were thereby spared the constant nomadic wandering of their Eurasian counterparts, but at a price. Instead of having access to fresh meat throughout the year, they were confronted with periods of glut, when the migrating herds

9

came their way, combined with long months when the only food available to them was their cached and frozen supplies.

There were other animals to hunt on the North American tundra, including musk oxen weighing as much as 400 kilograms and even the occasional polar bear. In general the inland wastes above the treeline were the least hospitable of the three northern environments. Those who had to live off them without access to the resources of either forest or sea were hard-pressed to survive at the best of times.

Even at high northern latitudes, the coasts provided a much better range of possibilities. The seas are plankton-rich, supporting a wide variety of marine life. They offer a rich harvest of seals and walrus that in winter can be hunted as they surface to take in air at breathing holes in the ice. There are fish, including the polar cod and the Arctic char, once the ice melts in summer, when the cliffs teem with ducks, gulls, geese and sea birds of many kinds. In some spots – particularly in northwestern Alaska and Greenland – whales are another crucial resource, traditionally hunted with harpoons from open boats called *umiak* and supplying entire communities with meat and blubber. In addition the coast-dwellers – including the coastal Chukchi of Siberia and the Aleut of the Aleutian Islands, as well as the Inuit peoples of Alaska, Canada and Greenland – have access to the tundra hunting-grounds inland, permitting them to live a semi-sedentary life.

Yet even if the resources were there to permit survival, the northern environment was never one to encourage large-scale settlement. People had to learn to live in the Arctic world, and the first settlers did so somewhere far back in the mists of prehistory. Most were probably small, dark-complexioned people of Mongoloid type – the Chukchi are thought to be their descendants. In the European north, the Saami of Lapland still speak a language originating in western Siberia, but like their linguistically related cousins the Finns and Hungarians, have gradually come to resemble Europeans through intermarriage.

The first settlers of the Arctic were probably big-game hunters, following wandering herds of reindeer, bison and wild horses as well as of mammoths, which may have survived on Russia's Wrangel Island until as late as 1000BC. They lived in quickly constructed houses made by excavating pits about thirty centimetres deep and two or three metres in diameter that they ringed with a frame of branches or mammoth bones. To these they lashed furs and skins, weighting them around the base with stones or sods. The floors were carpeted with more furs, leaving room only for a central hearth. The largest and most elaborate shelters were built at the start of winter, when they settled down in sheltered sites equipped with caches of meat naturally refrigerated by the ice and snow. As for iglus – the familiar ice-houses seen in some parts of North America – they were unknown in Siberia except among the Kerek people who did not have a reliable supply of wood and hides.

The First Americans

These nomadic hunters were unwittingly to leave a major mark on history, for they were to be the first discoverers and settlers of America. They achieved this giant leap by doing no more than following their usual habits. Many scholars believe that sometime in the last Ice Age their northwards drift brought them to the farthermost tip of Siberia at a time when glaciation had lowered sea-levels, creating a land-bridge across what is now the Bering Strait between Russia and Alaska. The travelling herds drew them inexorably into this great corridor, perhaps as much as 1,500 kilometres wide at its fullest extent. Finding little shelter in its wind-swept expanses, the game wandered on towards Alaska's Brooks Range, drawing the small hunter-gatherer groups, probably made up of no more than thirty to fifty individuals each, on into a new and uninhabited continent.

Controversy surrounds the question of when they made the crossing. In the past, the tendency was to push the date further and further back, sometimes as far as 30,000BC or more. More

CASPIAN SEA

JAPAN

• Vladivostok

Udegei

Nanai

Nivkhi

Lake Baikal

Khant

BLACK SEA

Evenk

SIBERIA

Evenk

Ket

Sakha (Yakut)

Evenk • Yakutsk

Evenk

Nenets

Even

Nganasan

Sakha (Yakut)

FINLAND

KAMCHATKA

Saami

SWEDEN

NORWAY

Koryak

Aleutian Islands

ARCTIC OCEAN

•

North Pole

Chukchi
**Siberian Yupik
(Eskimo)**

ICELAND

Aleut

Bering Strait

Inupiat

Yupik **Koyukon**

Tanaina

ALASKA

GREENLAND

*Kalaallit
(Inuit)*

*Kalaallit
(Inuit)*

**Mackenzie
Inuit**

*Kalaallit
(Inuit)*

**Victoria
Island**

*Iglulik
Inuit*

CANADA

Baffin Island

Copper Inuit

*Baffinland
Inuit*

Dogrib

**Netsilik
Inuit**

Kaska

**Caribou
Inuit**

Hudson Bay

**Labrador
Inuit**

*Naskapi
Montagnais*

Cree

Cree

■ Uninhabitable ice sheets

Tundra

Taiga

— Arctic Circle

The Peoples of the Arctic

The Arctic is varied in its physical
conditions and diverse population, the
key elements of which are shown here.

Preserving Life's Vital Provisions

As hunting was such an unpredictable pursuit, storing food against hard times was a crucial survival skill in the far north – and one in which the climate lent a vital helping hand.

An *ulu*, a tool used by Inuit women for butchering meat, scraping blubber from skin, sewing and other tasks.

For hunting peoples like the Inuit and the coastal Chukchi, migrating whales, caribou and other creatures were an essential food source. It was therefore paramount that these people found ways of storing the surplus meat to provide for the lean times that inevitably followed.

In the far north the game could simply be gutted and cached under rocks or blocks of ice, but in more southerly latitudes it had first to be sliced up and dried for two or three days; the strips were then put in special bags made of seal blubber and stored away from direct sunlight. In Alaska food was cached in cellars dug down into the permafrost, natural deep-freezes in which it kept for as long as three years.

None of these methods was entirely satisfactory, however, and some putrefaction did occur. The northerners learned to accept this, even developing a predilection for game that was unacceptably high by most other people's standards. Even more of an acquired taste, though, were such long-matured dishes as the Polar Inuit delicacy called *kiviaq* for which little auks were sewn complete with beaks and feathers into a blubber-lined sealskin sack for six months, fermented and then eaten raw.

recently, however, scientists have questioned these claims and the handful of radiocarbon dates on which they were mostly based. In the light of fresh evidence, opinion now tends to favour a date of not much before 12,000BC for the first penetration, though this too is open to challenge.

What is generally accepted is that the first Americans found their way south blocked by glaciers. When they found a way through, it was down narrow corridors: one along the Mackenzie River in what is now Canada's Northwest Territories, another possibly around Alaska's western coast. Some of the peoples who followed the game south as the Ice Age receded eventually doubled back to become the ancestors of such northern Indian peoples as the Cree and the Montagnais.

Meanwhile, important developments were under way back on the Eurasian landmass. The reindeer had become partly domesticated, and the peoples who had come to depend on it had settled into an annual cycle that involved following the big herds from their winter shelter in the forests to spring calving grounds on the tundra. They continued to hunt and trap other game, but the big deer increasingly provided for most of their needs: meat and fat for food, hides for clothing and shelter, sinews for thread, bones and antlers for tools. They also served as beasts of burden, carrying the tents the Chukchi call *yaranga*.

In time some of the tundra herders got into the habit of moving to the seashore for a few months each summer. There they exploited the rich food resources, hunting seals and walrus, fishing for migrating salmon and collecting birds' eggs, seaweed and shellfish. In so doing, they were developing the characteristic features of a lifestyle that would in time become indissolubly associated with the Inuit (Eskimo) peoples.

The Coming of the Eskimos

The word "Eskimo" needs some comment, as it has recently fallen out of fashion. For many years scholars traced its derivation to an Algonquin word meaning "eater of raw flesh", which Eskimos themselves understandably considered derogatory. As a result, Canadian Eskimos in the 1970s chose to substitute the term "Inuit", which simply means "people" in the Inuit language, Inuktitut.

Yet the change has caused problems for historians, for not all Eskimos are Inuktitut speakers; a substantial minority in Alaska and Siberia speak the Yupik language, while the ethnically related inhabitants of the Aleutian Islands use Aleut and those in Greenland call themselves Kalaallit. In addition, recent linguistic research suggests that the word "Eskimo" might not be derived from the Algonquian term after all, but rather from a Montagnais word meaning "snowshoe trapper" – an epithet with no negative connotations. For historical purposes, then, "Eskimo" remains the only word to describe the ethnic group as a whole and is so used in this chapter, even though elsewhere in the book the term "Inuit" is usually preferred, reflecting present-day sensitivities.

Whatever their name, the ancestors of the Eskimo peoples seem to have been relatively late arrivals over the Bering Strait. They almost certainly came after the land-bridge had been submerged as sea levels rose with the ending of the Ice Age, an event that probably occurred sometime around 11,000BC. The first evidence of their presence comes from the Aleutian Islands between Siberia and Alaska, suggesting that they made their way eastwards by boat – no doubt the skin-covered *umiak*, holding as many as eight people, that were still in use for whaling into the twentieth century. Alternatively, they could have walked across the pack ice that still sometimes jams the wide strait in very cold winters.

The first definite evidence of their presence on the American mainland comes from about 2000BC, the date of the earliest Eskimo artifacts so far unearthed in North America. The link with Asia, their original home, is clear enough, not just in the nature of the objects found but also in similarities between the Inuit, Yupik and Aleut languages and those of Siberian peoples on the other side of the strait, notably Chukchi and Kamchadal. No similar correspondence has been noted with American Indian tongues.

As latecomers, the Eskimos' ancestors found the coastal areas at which they first arrived long settled by earlier immigrants. But there was virgin territory to the north and east. The Ice Age's lingering grip had been slow to loosen on the Arctic coastline of Alaska and Canada. It was not until about 3000BC that the ice sheet eventually receded under the impact of global warming. As it did so, it opened up a corridor across the far north that the newcomers were quick to exploit.

Archaeologists have uncovered a shadowy prehistory for these proto-Eskimos, giving different groups evocative names on the basis of the limited finds made at a handful of scattered sites. As they tell it, the Old Whaling People, whose deposits of whalebone and harpoon tips have been dug up at a single site at Cape Krusenstern in northwestern Alaska, gave way to the Small Tool People, who

Walrus ivory carving from the Piutak culture, Seward peninsula, c.AD500. The central motif is a bear and the protruding teeth behind suggest this is a comb, probably for cleaning skins.

13

spread rapidly eastwards across Canada to Greenland. By about 800BC, the Small Tool tradition evolved into the Dorset culture, so called after Cape Dorset on Baffin Island where its remains were first found. Dorset people are identified by the distinctive way in which they shaped their tools and by the elegant carvings of humans and animals that sometimes adorned them.

Despite the differences in the detail of their tools and utensils, these cultures had much in common. First and foremost, they nearly all featured a lifestyle primarily directed towards the sea. By looking to the coast for a living, the Eskimos' ancestors made a culturally crucial decision, turning their back on the deer-hunting and herding with which their predecessors in Siberia must have been familiar and adopting instead a mainly marine lifestyle, hunting seal, walrus and whales. Other shared features included toggled harpoons, skin boats, blubber lamps and semi-subterranean dwellings – all elements that the immigrants would have brought with them from Asia.

Before long there were Eskimo groups stretched all the way across the north of America and on into Greenland, a distance of some 5,000 kilometres that made them one of the most far-flung aboriginal populations in the world. Throughout their territory, they shared the same basic resources: snow and ice, which they used to build iglus and food caches; skins for clothing, tents and boots; bone, antler and ivory that they carved with great delicacy into weapons, tools and needles; and stone, which served to make large implements such as oil lamps and cooking pots as well as cutting edges for knives and scrapers. Timber was in short supply, as they mostly lived above the treeline; what little was available came mainly in the form of driftwood. Sometime in the first millennium AD metal also made its first appearance. Iron came to Alaska through trade from metal-working peoples to the south, while naturally occuring copper was discovered by the inhabitants of northern Canada's Victoria Island and the adjoining mainland. These people became known as the Copper Eskimos.

High-Latitude Living

In social terms, the defining feature of the Eskimo lifestyle was also inherited from the Asian past. This was the annual cycle of movement between camps, which usually involved gathering in relatively large settlements for the winter months then splitting up into smaller groups for the summer hunting. Within these communities, the main social component was the extended family. There was little in the way of social hierarchies or structured lines of authority, for the Eskimos always retained the anarchic freedom of the hunting lifestyle in which the principal constraints are imposed by nature, not by man.

A new element entered the cultural mix in about AD1000, when the Dorset peoples were displaced or absorbed by the Thule culture, the direct precursor of modern Inuit society. The Thule Eskimos introduced the dog-sled, previously unknown, and gave increased importance to whaling. By that time they were not only firmly established all across the American Arctic and Greenland, but had also moved back across the Bering Strait into Siberia, on whose northeasternmost tip a small community survives to this day.

Despite the obvious similarities linking the Eskimo cultures from Greenland to Siberia, there was still room for wide differences in lifestyle. One split was between the different language groups. Others were linked to the environment. For example, the sea rarely freezes around the Aleutian Islands, so the Aleut practised a more conventional form of hunting and fishing than those who hunted amid the ice of the Arctic region.

The Yupik-speakers of southwestern Alaska also had traditions that were quite distinct from those of the Inuit and Inupiat to the north. The coast there is particularly rich in marine life, including bowhead whales migrating annually to their calving grounds in the Arctic Ocean. There are rivers well stocked with fish and inland plains rich in berries and edible grasses as well as game.

Such abundance led to the development of villages in which populations running into the hundreds stayed for as much as ten months of the year. Their solidly constructed, semi-subterranean homes were often built of logs, for the treeline was rarely far away. In these permanent settlements they developed a rich community life which revolved around the men's houses – communal dwellings where the menfolk would spend weeks on end in winter, eating, sleeping, repairing their old hunting equipment and preparing new gear for the season ahead. Food was brought in by the women, who lived in smaller sod houses built around the larger building and spent their time preparing skins, making clothes and boots, and looking after the children.

In the evenings, the women would sometimes join the men for sessions of singing and story-telling or for lively sporting contests in which individuals would show off their wrestling or gymnastic skills. In some of the larger villages, these winter gatherings crystallized over the years into

Below: A wooden model of a *qasgiq*, or community house, from the lower Yukon area. The correct configuration of four men and a woman are shown performing a *pualla* dance. A similar ritual celebration is captured in the early 20th-century photograph (right). Drums are again a key feature.

large festivals (see page 108). In extreme cases the entire winter season was turned into an elaborate ceremonial round in which every element reflected in some way the prevailing preoccupation with the food supply and the hunt. One of the best-documented examples was the Bladder Festival, for which the bladders of all the seals killed in the past hunting season were welcomed into the men's house as honoured guests. They remained there for several days before being ceremonially returned to the sea from which they had come, where, it was hoped, they would be reborn as new seals which would once again give themselves willingly to the villagers' harpoons.

The situation was very different in the great wastes of central Canada, where the density of the population was only one-tenth to one-fiftieth of the Yupik's and much of the year was spent on the move in search of scarce game. This was the only area in which the iglu, constructed of blocks of ice, was the standard winter dwelling, for despite popular preconceptions only about five per cent of the total Eskimo population ever used these as their main living-quarters; elsewhere they only served as temporary shelters, usually built by hunters when they were out on long trips.

It was also the region where the threat of famine loomed largest. Starvation always played a central part in the Eskimo imagination, understandably given their day-to-day dependence on unreliable food supplies, yet for most groups it was more a fear than a reality. But for relatively isolated communities like the Caribou Eskimos of the Barren Grounds west of Hudson Bay, the danger was ever-present. Life in such circumstances could seem very precarious indeed.

Even in the better-provided regions, Eskimos, like all the northern peoples, had to become expert at maximizing all available resources. They showed particular ingenuity in coping with the Arctic cold. Their clothing took advantage of the insulating properties of the hides of the beasts they hunted. Underclothes were made of eider-duck skins with the feathers still on them. For pants and parkas they used caribou hides, whose hollow hairs provided a natural form of cavity insulation. Boots would be made with a double skin to trap the heat, and were lined with moss; hoods were fringed with wolverine fur, which has the unique property of not trapping breath moisture in icy particles.

Similar savoir-faire went into the building of houses, which were dug down deep into the earth and provided with passageways sunk lower than the hut floor to keep the warm air inside. Body heat

Wood, leather and fur figure of an Udegei shaman riding to the spirit world on his guide, probably a Siberian tiger, *c.*1900. It would have protected a shaman on his journey.

The Birth of Skiing

The origins of skiing are lost in the mists of time, for from early on skis were an essential means of transport. In Scandinavia they date back more than 5,000 years.

The oldest skis so far discovered come from bogs in Sweden and Finland and are thought to be between 4,000 and 5,000 years old. The first known depiction of skiers also comes from Scandinavia, in the form of a rock carving found near the Arctic Circle in Norway that has been dated to 2000BC.

As far as collected evidence suggests, some of the earliest skis were short and broad, more nearly resembling the snowshoes which are also thought to have been in use in various parts of northern Asia several thousand years ago. Similar footwear is still used in North America today, as it permits hunters and trappers to move across soft snow without sinking and getting stuck. In general, however, long, ski-like footwear is best for travelling at speed in open country, whereas shorter, rounder designs are more suitable in rough or wooded terrain. For longer distances sledges and teams of huskies are favoured.

Siberian skis, like these 19th-century examples, used reindeer-leg fur or sealskin to give a good grip on the ice.

helped too; whole families would sleep on a communal sleeping platform stretching all the way across the back of the dwelling, covered with fox and polar-bear skins that served both as under-sheets and blankets.

In these enclosed, smoky dwellings, the Inuit story-tellers passed on the tales that had kept northern listeners enthralled for countless generations. Similar stories were told not just in America but by other Arctic peoples over the seas in Scandinavia, Siberia and Greenland too. There were marked similarities not just between the folk-tales told across the northern latitudes but also in religious beliefs. Throughout the Arctic regions these were animistic; people thought of the natural world as filled with powerful spirits with whom it was necessary to negotiate if they were not to take offence at the human inhabitants of the world.

Also common to all the northern cultures was the figure of the shaman, a specialist in communicating with the spirit world; indeed, the word itself is a Tungus term, introduced into other European languages via Russian. Everywhere, shamans used rhythms beaten out on special drums to induce the trances in which they went on their psychic voyages. The use of spirit helpers whose assistance was necessary to diagnose and cure sickness or undo the damage done by taboo infringements was another shared feature.

There were also marked similarities in the world-views of all the Arctic peoples. Nearly all believed in a multi-layered universe, with the human world sandwiched between multiple spirit realms; there were varying opinions, though, as to the exact number of these worlds and whether the more desirable ones lay above or below. Human beings too were often thought to have several different souls, one of them perhaps attached to the name an individual was given.

Obviously in an area the size of the Arctic and subarctic, there were also significant local differences. Some Siberian peoples thought that the

17

goodwill of potent spirits known as "animal masters" was essential for success in any major enterprise such as a dangerous voyage or a hunt. Others especially venerated a bear spirit, thought of as the Lord of the Forest, and took care to show due respect to the flesh-and-blood bears that he protected. The Inuit gave central importance to a Sea Mother, herself an animal mistress controlling all the creatures living under the waves (see page 58). Other beings accorded special status were the spirit of the moon and Sila, the Inuit spirit who controlled the winds and weather.

For countless generations the patterns of northern life repeated themselves almost unchanged, following the rhythm of the seasons. Century after century, the hunters went out in search of seal or walrus over the sea-ice or trekked inland on the trail of caribou or musk ox as their fathers, grandfathers and great-grandfathers had done before them. Their skills, their weapons, even their homes and clothes changed little from those known to hunter-gatherers of the earliest times, although skilfully adapted to the special circumstances of the far northern environment.

The harsh climate and difficult terrain seemed to preserve those who had learned to master them in a time warp, cut off from the rest of humankind, which went about its business in complete ignorance of their very existence. But the isolation was not to last. Eventually the rest of the world penetrated the northern fastnesses, with consequences for the native peoples that are still being felt today.

The Outside World Intrudes

Among the first to come into contact with their southern neighbours were the Saami of Lapland, whose existence was known to the Roman historian Tacitus as well as to the ninth-century English monarch Alfred the Great. Throughout the Middle Ages there were local clashes with settlers from the south, driven northwards by the same need for new land that spawned the Viking voyages. Over the centuries the Saami would become a minority in their own country, stretched across the modern nations of Norway, Sweden and Finland as well as the northwestern corner of Russia. Yet many have retained their reindeer-herding

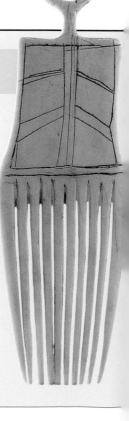

TIMELINE	30,000–800BC	800BC–AD1300
For millennia vast tracts of the Arctic were home to peoples who continued to live according to their age-old traditions. These lifestyles, however, were interrupted by the arrival of traders and explorers from Europe and Imperial Russia. The area was never to be the same again. But despite the ravages of disease and economic exploitation, indigenous cultures now have the chance to rebuild themselves again.	**c.30,000–12,000BC** Peoples from Siberia used the land-bridge to cross the Bering Strait and began to populate the Arctic region. **c.11,000BC** The first Eskimo peoples began hunting in the Aleutian islands. **c.9000–6000BC** The earliest settlements were created in the region. Coastal hunters began to adapt to exploit the bountiful marine resources. **c.3000BC** Melting of ice sheets allowed the spread of the Arctic population northwards and eastwards across present-day Canada. **c.800BC** The small tool tradition of the Dorset culture emerged around Cape Dorset on Baffin Island.	**c.330BC** Pytheas became the first human to record his exploration of the Arctic in writing when he travelled to the north coast of Norway. **c.AD900–1000** Period of cooling in the Arctic region. **986** Erik the Red led the first Viking expedition to Greenland. **c.1000** Dorset peoples were displaced by Thule culture, precursor of modern Inuit. Emergence of metal-working in the region. **1250** Eskimos encountered Greenland Norsemen.

Miniature mask possibly used by a shaman, Dorset culture, c.500BC.

Ivory comb with a stylized human figure, c.AD1000.

life today, even as others compromised with the incomers by abandoning the nomadic life for the settled existence of smallholding by the sea.

For a time, the vast distances of Russia protected the country's northern peoples from encroachment. It was hard for outsiders to penetrate their remote fastnesses as there were no roads to bring them. Until the Trans-Siberian Railway was built early in the twentieth century, the only way to travel from the Urals to the Pacific was by horseback along rough tracks, and the journey took more than two years.

Even so, the north's long isolation was shattered in the years following 1581, when the tsar sent a band of Cossacks across the mountains in search of sable pelts – the world's most precious fur. The fur trade was for Siberia what gold was for the Klondike; and in the wake of that first expedition dozens more followed. Within fifty years the intruders reached the Pacific, building a chain of forts from Omsk to Vladivostok on the way.

The Cossacks regarded the indigenous peoples they encountered as natives to be traded with or taxed for their furs, much as the Hudson's Bay

Company did when they arrived in Canada eager to exploit the riches they found. Only in a few areas was there a pattern of genocide, as in the American West, since the Russians did not generally want to seize land for their own agriculture or ranching. Few of the 100 or more ethnic groups believed to have been in existence at that time were in much of a position to offer substantial opposition, divided as they mostly were into small nomadic clans. Only the Chukchi put up serious resistance, defeating several military expeditions sent against them. But eventually they, like the others, were absorbed into the Russian administrative system that gradually spread across the conquered territories. By 1900 only about twenty-five separate peoples were left.

1300–1800	1800–PRESENT DAY

c.1400 The last remnants of the Dorset culture, still living in northern Quebec and Labrador, began to die out.
c.1450–1850 A period known as the Little Ice Age during which plunging temperatures forced settlers out of the most northerly regions.
1497 John Cabot led the first serious search for the Northwest Passage.
1500 Norse settlers deserted Greenland after failure of their farming techniques.
1576 British explorer Martin Frobisher set sail to discover the Northwest Passage.
1581 Russian tsar sent Cossacks eastwards into Siberia in search of valuable sable pelts.
c.1600 Weather deteriorated throughout the Arctic as the "Little Ice Age" peaked.
1799 The Russian American Company was granted monopoly trading rights in Alaska by the Russian crown. Russian influence began to spread throughout Siberia.

c.1820 Missionaries began to spread Christianity throughout the Arctic.
1867 Russia sold Alaska to the USA. Schools and health clinics were closed and the region became a forgotten outpost.
1917 The Russian revolution initiated a programme of education and Communist indoctrination in Siberia.
c.1970 Beginnings of movement to reassert the values of Inuit culture.
1999 The Inuit of Nunavut were given self-government by Canada.

Jessie Oonark's Sunface and Birdcatchers, *textile art from the Baker Lake area, mixes shaman and snowmobiles, old and new.*

Royal Navy officers John Ross and William Parry trade metal for walrus tusks with Cape York Eskimos during their expedition to Greenland in 1818. Lithograph from a drawing by the explorers' Inuit guide, Hans Zakaeus.

Although Russian Orthodox missionaries had some success in converting the tsar's new subjects, for the most part administrators were content to tax them in furs and other produce but otherwise leave them undisturbed. As a result, their lifestyle changed relatively little.

That policy changed with the Russian Revolution, when with the best of intentions the country's new masters decided to extend the benefits of Soviet citizenship to their comrades in the far north. The consequence was a marked improvement in living standards, but also a much more intrusive policy of assimilation. People who had never seen horse-drawn carts, let alone cars or trains, suddenly became used to the sight of

aeroplanes bringing administrators and ethnologists. One Chukchi writer subsequently joked that after the Soviet takeover the typical family came to consist of "father, mother, two children, as well as over there in the corner of the hut the researcher".

Education was introduced, and young people were taken off to boarding schools where they learned about a world very different from the one their parents had known. One result was the opening up of a huge generation gap between a younger generation, brought up as Soviet citizens, and their hunting or reindeer-herding parents. The pace of change here was particularly brutal.

In the Inuit territories of Greenland and America, exposure to the outside world came rather more gradually. The Icelandic sagas suggest that Viking explorers encountered Eskimos both in Greenland and in Vinland, their name for North America; indeed, the hostile reception they received there was one of the reasons why they decided not to establish an American colony. In their strange skin clothing, Eskimos were also objects of curiosity to the pioneers of the Renaissance Age of Exploration; Martin Frobisher even brought a family he seized on Baffin Island back to the court of Queen Elizabeth I, where they soon died of Western diseases to which they had no acquired immunity.

The first large-scale outside disruption in America, however, came not directly from settlers but from Indian peoples driven northwards by the Europeans further south, who were seeking furs much as the Russians were in Siberia at the same time. It struck at a bad time for the Eskimos, for they had recently been adversely affected by a deterioration of the northern climate associated with the so-called "Little Ice Age" that peaked in the seventeenth century. This episode of global cooling was not much worse than an inconvenience in southerly latitudes, but up above the treeline it made the already harsh conditions even worse. As food resources shrank, rivalries increased between the groups exploiting them, and a wave of feuding and local wars engulfed the Eskimo lands. The arrival of Indians armed with guns obtained from the white settlers made a difficult situation worse and led to many years of armed skirmishing.

Then in the nineteenth century direct links with the white man were forged as missionaries and fur traders arrived in Eskimo lands. At first the fur trade brought unaccustomed prosperity, and some groups became completely dependent on it. By the time fashions changed and the market for furs declined, they had lost many of their traditional skills and found that they were barely able to support themselves.

Worse, unfamiliar diseases had come with the outsiders, and epidemics of influenza, diphtheria, polio and tuberculosis cut swathes through the indigenous population. A further blow came when southern hunters equipped with rifles decimated the caribou herds on which the northerners had traditionally depended. In Canada at least, the result was a disastrous decline. When the condition of the Canadian Inuit was investigated in 1958, one in eight of the population was found to be infected with tuberculosis, the infant mortality rate was higher than one in four and life expectancy was just twenty-four years.

Since then, the material condition of most northern peoples has improved considerably, though sometimes at the cost of cutting links with the traditional past. In recent decades living standards have risen almost everywhere except perhaps in Russia, and most have attained some degree of self-rule (see page 136). Yet these advances have not necessarily been matched by a greater sense of well-being. From being unchallenged masters of their own isolated environment, the Arctic's indigenous inhabitants now find themselves second-class citizens in a larger world not of their making, in which they often have difficulty finding jobs or a meaningful social role. Throughout the northern lands the sense of disorientation is palpable, and rates of alcoholism and suicide are high.

To re-establish links with the past, some young people are now turning back to the tales and traditions of earlier times. In a society that is changing rapidly around them, they find a sense of continuity in the old stories of the struggle for survival and shamanic soul quests. They draw strength from the heroism of their ancestors and breathe new life into the mythologies of the past – and by so doing revitalize their culture. For them and for a wider world, the old lore still has much to offer.

Ivory walrus tusks have always been prized Inuit gifts. This pipe provided a valuable piece for trade with Europeans.

21

THE SACRED WHALE

From the very earliest times the whale has dominated the material life and the imagination of the Inuit. The many species of whale that lived around the seas of the Arctic provided the region's first hunters with an invaluable resource that catered for nearly all their basic needs: from food to oil for burning and baleen for making tools – and, in a land where there was a shortage of wood, even bone frameworks for housing. This all-encompassing use of whale products meant that the creature became a central symbol for seaboard communities. The rituals surrounding the hunt were especially prominent during the spring and autumn migrations. In the Bering Sea area, myths told how the great cetacean was not just an animal but even formed the land itself. Through the ubiquity of its physical and symbolic forms the spirit of the whale infused all things.

Left: The physical and spiritual presence of the whale haunts even the land. These whale ribs at the historic site at Masik, in Chukotka, Siberia, have been used as a framework for a house.

Far right: A special whale-shaped box carved to hold the blades to be fitted to a whaling harpoon. Placing the blades inside a symbol of their intended prey was a way of placating whale spirits, ensuring a successful hunt.

Right: This harpoon head would have held a barb or blade and was attached by a line to a lance thrown by one of the whalers from the boat. The hunter has carved a wolf onto the implement in order to invoke that animal's cunning and ensure a clean and quick kill.

Right: While shamans struggled with the dangers of the spirit world, hunters had to brave the open seas and the hazards posed by both the elements and the whales themselves, for their huge bulk could easily crush the boats the Inuit used to hunt in. These fishermen, from St Lawrence Island in the Bering Sea, are sailing in an *umiak,* a boat made from driftwood and walrus hides. The boat could be rowed but sails were used for long-distance journeys.

Left: Most animal-mask dances were performed to propitiate the spirit of the animal that was to be hunted – and ensure an abundance of quarry. This was also one of the shaman's most important functions. Wearing this ceremonial mask, a shaman from the Kuskokwim region in Alaska would have consorted with the spirits of whales and sought to guide a school of them towards the harpoons of his community's hunters.

SHADOWS OF CREATION

While the successors of Columbus cut a swathe through Central and South America, tearing open a luxuriant Eden and cracking a treasure-house of incalculable wealth, their counterparts further north were having an altogether harder time of it. The fabled Northwest Passage, which was supposed to lead to Cathay's immeasurable riches, was proving maddeningly elusive and, as for America itself, the new-found continent was, at these frigid latitudes, just about as unlike the Caribbean coast as could be imagined. The ambitious French navigator Jacques Cartier, an early European visitor to Labrador in 1534, was expecting similarly lush pastures, but instead found "stones and wild craggs, and a place fit for wild beasts". "To be short," he concluded, "I believe that this was the land that God allotted to Cain."

Cartier's appalled reaction still resonates today. Nowhere has nature proved more indomitable than it has in the circumpolar lands, where darkness reigns through half the year and a grudging earth unlocks only a few scant surface inches of soil for a pitifully short time each summer. "These men may very well and truly be called wild," recorded Cartier of the region's sixteenth-century population, "for I think all that they had together, besides their boats and nets was not worth five souce."

Yet the indigenous population, had they known of it, would have found his horror puzzling. Their wealth may not have been readily convertible into European currency, but they possessed all the knowledge and skills they needed for life amid the ice-floes. The world which seemed so bleak and unforgiving to the visitor yielded them food and clothing, although not always readily. They looked to nature to furnish what they required and they saw no need to accumulate possessions, which in any case would only have hindered their nomadic lifestyle. The dreadful solitude the southerner found here would have astonished a people closely adapted to their environment and to whom every animal, bird and fish was known along with their attendant ancestral spirits. They certainly would not have recognized the empty place described by the terrified Cartier, for they embraced these wild plains of snow and negotiated with them to survive, and even found within their cold and hostile bounds images of great wonder and delight.

Opposite: **European explorers found the Arctic desolate and terrifying. To the Inuit who lived there, however, these were lands of infinite subtlety and wonder.**

Below: **An Inuit soapstone carving of a seal, c.20th century. For skilled hunters, the Arctic was rich in game.**

A World Unseen

There was much more to the Arctic landscape than endless floes of ice and sea, for the Inuit and others believed that this visible world was only one of several parallel realities. But these hidden spirit realms could be accessed with the aid of special guides.

In common with nomadic herdsmen and hunters throughout the world's remaining wilder regions, the peoples of the Arctic saw their world through the glass of shamanism. An ancient creed which by its very nature existed in myriad local variations, shamanism regarded everyday reality as but the physical manifestation of a more elaborate unseen universe. Every visible thing, according to this view, was a pointer to parallel levels beyond, a window upon worlds rich with the spirits of

Stone figure of a shaman by Eric Niuqtuk, c.1970. The Inuit believed that shamans could transform themselves into animals.

animals, birds and plants, and of human ancestors. High above the sky, beneath the earth or below the bottom of the sea lay other skies, earths and seas with their own spirit inhabitants. Some Siberian peoples recognized no fewer than thirteen distinct realms. At one level or another in this elaborate cosmos, every living thing – from the past as well as the present – had its place.

Although concealed from normal sight, these planes could be explored in the trance of the shaman, that man or woman who in every Inuit community served as spiritual guide. Shamans had the power to wander at will from one world to another on behalf of their people, seeking the spirits' help in their every undertaking and beseeching their pardon for any offence. No significant step would be taken without the advice of the immortals, solicited by the shaman: no journey or hunt would be embarked on without their blessing. Scarcity of game or adverse weather, illness or infertility, on the other hand, might all mark displeasure in the spirit world. It was the shaman who ascertained what reasons lay behind such misfortunes, and advised on how to restore harmony with the spirits.

In some cultures the shaman soared aloft on an eagle or dived on a fish's back to reach these other worlds. Among the Siberian peoples he might ride a reindeer, climb a column of smoke, or simply walk. In many traditions the shaman had to pass through a narrow aperture in the sky to gain access to the realms beyond. But these parallel levels, though invisible from this one, were not always seen as remote from it: hence the tale told by the Chukchi of northeastern Siberia about the eight brothers who went out whaling one day, and strayed across such a boundary unawares.

26

The Eight Brothers

Harpooning a much bigger whale than they had encountered before, the brothers struggled long and hard to kill their catch, while a brisk wind carried them ever further out to sea. Too late they decided to cut the whale loose and make a last-minute run for home: night fell to find them far out of sight of land. Adrift in the dark of midnight, they were just giving themselves up for lost when their boat bumped up on a sandy shore. Such a landfall was quite unexpected, of course, but they were in no mood to question their good fortune. Then their eldest brother went off to find fresh water, but when he failed to return after many hours it occurred to them that something must be amiss. One by one the brothers walked off into the dark land beyond and failed to return, until at last the youngest brother was left alone, desperately thirsty, yet rooted to the spot by fear. Fortunately, he was befriended by a star spirit from high in the heavens. It explained that he and his brothers had washed up in another, parallel world. Here dwelled the dead whose spirits hungered for mortal souls: they had already seized his brothers', and would not rest till they had his too. If he followed the star's instructions, however, he might yet make it safely home. So, steered by this shining guide above, he set off across the sand until he at last came upon a large hut in a prosperous-looking village.

The master welcomed him kindly, bidding him enter and eat from the huge cooking pot that dominated his home. Listening courteously to the boy's story, he pushed the cauldron to one side: underneath was a hole through which he invited the astonished boy to peer. Far below were his parents, and all the other kin he had left behind, celebrating some joyful festival. He burst into tears, and the revelries beneath were broken up by the unexpected rain.

Touched by his grief, the master offered to return him to his family, asking only that a dog be sacrificed to him for his pains. And so, shouldering the cauldron aside once more, he lowered the boy down through the hole on a rope, to be joyfully reunited with his parents.

His father resolved to sacrifice a reindeer in thanksgiving but when the boy insisted that the family's favourite dog be offered, the old man refused to allow it. A fine buck was therefore sacrificed instead and the festivities continued far into the night until everyone settled down to sleep. Next morning when they awoke, they found the boy's body lying cold as stone: through his father's ingratitude he had been lost a second time.

The skill of Inuit hunters is depicted in a 1974 woodcut by Bernard Tuglamena titled *One Chance*. The whale-hunt was a central feature of life in the Arctic, both spiritually and materially.

The Earth Emerges

Every Arctic people had its own version of how the Earth came to be created. One feature that united many of these tales, however, was the belief that creation began with a first, flawed world which was then drowned by a cataclysmic flood.

A long time ago an old Inuit woman called Arnaruluk lived in the most northerly part of Greenland. She told many great tales about the creation of the Arctic and according to her, the first Earth fell from the sky. Soil, stones and mountains, all cascaded down, and as the dust cleared the first men and women came crawling from the ground. But theirs was a wretched existence, for they dwelled in darkness and lived on a diet of dirt.

Such was their great ignorance, however, that they did not know how to die. Their numbers grew and grew until the Earth was crowded to the point of collapse – and as the ground began to disintegrate, a fearful flood swept across the Earth, washing away every sign of human life.

When the waters finally receded, it became apparent that a few people had survived: shocked, and perhaps made wiser, by their experience. Life could not go on as it had before, said some more enterprising souls; surely it would be worth enduring death in return for light. And so it came about. The world was granted sunlight and seasons, though in return men and women had to accept that their lives had to end. They had no cause to regret the contract, though, for now they could hunt game, build boats and lead lives transformed by light; and even in death they were to become things of light, not darkness. For when men and women died now, their souls took flight to Heaven where, transfigured by radiance, they twinkled down on the Earth as shining stars.

Further south in the Canadian homeland of the Cree, in subarctic Ontario, a different tale was told. As the Sandy Lake Cree would have it, the creator was called Wee-sa-kay-jac. One day he found his life's work threatened when evil spirits began to dig down into the earth to release all the water contained within it. The resulting flood spread throughout the world, covering forests and drowning animals. The few survivors were finally forced to take refuge together on a single scrap of higher ground that had until that time escaped the rising tide. Looking around this little island, and seeing it shrinking all the time, Wee-sa-kay-jac knew he had to think quickly. He scanned the available resources and took stock of his companions – then detailed all the survivors to build a giant canoe, giving each animal their own instructions. Beavers felled great trees and the muskrats bound the logs together with strong, pliable roots. Then frogs caulked the hull with lumps of mud, while birds lined it warmly with grass and feathers. Just in time the boat was finished, and as the island disappeared it floated gently off with all its passengers safely aboard. And so it tacked to and fro across the waves for many months until the waters finally stopped rising.

Wee-sa-kay-jac now saw it was time to recreate the Earth. When he realized he had no clay from which to make it, he sent his companions down to retrieve some from the bottom of the sea. The beaver and the otter were drowned in the

A late 19th-century Aleut model of a kayak. In the tale of Wee-sa-kay-jac, it was one of these boats which helped the last remaining animals survive the flood. In the story of the three friends, however, a similar vessel led them into trouble (right).

attempt and so too was the muskrat. But when its body bobbed up to the surface, Wee-sa-kay-jac found between its claws a tiny trace of clay – enough for him to fashion a whole new world. He brought his three hapless divers back to life and, calling for a cooking pot, he boiled the clay for several hours. The clay grew and grew, over-spilling the sides of the pot until it had reached beyond the farthest horizon. Wee-sa-kay-jac then turned to the wolverine and commanded it to walk around the newly created Earth to ascertain its size. When it came back again no more than two days later, Wee-sa-kay-jac concluded that the world was still too small. He kept his clay cooking and then sent the scout out on a second expedition. When the animal was despatched for a third time, however, it failed to find its way back, so vast had the Earth become. Only then did Wee-sa-kay-jac deem his creation wide enough. The great creator then took a small lump of clay from the cooking pot, and from its shapeless form he fashioned the first man.

A Great House of Ice

Ever since they first set foot in the region, Arctic-dwellers have crossed the vast, snow-bound territories looking for new hunting grounds or natural resources. The lifestyle of the people was nomadic, the search for food dictated by the change of seasons and the migrations of prey. One blackly comic Inuit tale, however, carried its own wry warning about the dangers of a large, perilous landscape.

Three friends set out in their kayaks on a voyage of discovery, to determine the size and shape of the Earth around them. For three days and nights they paddled on, and they had long since left familiar territory behind when they saw rising before them an enormous ice-house, its roof flush against the very heavens. Seeing a door, the three men went in and, following the sheer white walls so as not to get lost in the vast interior, they worked their way round the endless dome – and round and round again. The entrance had vanished and, growing ever more agitated as they tramped on and on, they found themselves circling vainly through weeks and months, and even years.

His two companions had collapsed and died with exhaustion before the third friend finally located the door. But when he opened it, he emerged to find his kayak waiting, just as he had left it.

A stooped and wizened old man now, he made his way home and told his astonished kinsfolk with his dying breath: the Earth is nothing more than an enormous ice-house.

Mother of the World

For each story accounting for the creation of the world there seemed to be one describing how it was populated. But here, Arctic opinion was particularly divided. Some accounts claimed that man came first, others that humankind was nurtured by female guile.

Once, says an Inuit legend, there was only one woman in the world – and she was really only a man who had turned his male member inwards to form a womb. Her body was graceful and her face alluring, but living alone on the island, there was no one to be seduced by her charms.

In time, though, some male was sure to happen upon the remote, rocky island where Putu, or "Hole", lived, and one day a hunter did indeed put ashore on the beach below her hut. He could not believe his eyes when he saw this beautiful creature gazing down at him invitingly. With such a desirable mate at his side, he had no thought of ever leaving. Even his headman at home was not as privileged as he, the love-struck hunter crowed inwardly as he lay beside her. But before long that very headman set out in search of his missing subject.

Soon he had arrived at Putu's hut and, looking in, he saw the couple making love. He would have his share of this, he thought, and, waiting till the hunter and his mistress had fallen into a satisfied sleep, he grabbed the woman by the shoulders and started dragging her towards the door. Waking up, the hunter managed to seize her feet and a tug of war ensued in the course of which poor Putu snapped clean in two. The headman made off with her upper half while his rival had what was left of her from the waist down.

Each attempted to make good the missing sections from carved bear bones and walrus ivory, but back in the village the headman's consort gave rise to envy and enmity among the other men. She was torn in two, then four and so on until every man had a mate of some sort. None, however, proved as fertile as Putu's lower half which remained back on her island home, and bore the lucky hunter 600 handsome sons and daughters.

Crow the Maker and Game Mother

A myth of the Canadian Dene, by contrast, claims that Crow, the first creator, made women by the simple act of dressing men in feminine clothes. Unaccustomed to their role, these first women had no idea of how to produce children, and as the babies began to grow inside them they thought themselves ill. They were all for cutting their bellies open to remove the malignant growth until

A 19th-century hunting cap from the Bering Sea region. The carved ivory gull beaks, walrus heads and feathers encouraged the creatures created by the Game Mother to give themselves up willingly to the hunter.

30

Crow explained exactly what was happening. When their babies were born, he had to teach them to breast-feed, and then to wean their infants by letting them suck on pieces of fat, the Dene way.

Despite the obvious differences between them, the stories of Putu and Crow's wives share the view that woman derived from man, in the same way that the Bible tells that Eve grew from Adam's rib. Yet while many myths of the Arctic regions do start out from this premise, it is by no means universal, as the Inuit myth of the Game Mother makes clear.

In this story, all the animals are born from the loins of a human woman. First comes the moose, who is mistakenly equipped with sharp carnivore's teeth. The Game Mother calls him back, removes them and teaches the moose to eat marsh plants and twigs, to lick mud in search of salt and to shed his horns every so often. Next the caribou is born, and she introduces him to his diet of moss. The grizzly bear follows and, like the moose, he has cruel teeth. His mother calls him back too, hoping to remove them, but he refuses to return. So it goes on until the Game Mother has brought the entire animal kingdom into being.

The Toy People

In northeast Siberia, the Chukchi tell the tale of the Toy People, a powerful tribute to the creative force of woman. The story – very reminiscent of that of Sedna, the Sea Mother (see pages 58–59) – concerns a young girl whose father demands that she marry

An ivory figurine carved in a style typical of the Bering Strait Inuit. The Chukchi of northeast Siberia said that humankind was fashioned out of clay by a young girl who had fled her home to begin her life again.

an elderly neighbour. She refuses, insisting that she does not yet want to take a husband. Her father is unrelenting, however, and when she remains adamant, he orders her to leave the family home. Distraught, she seizes what she can find immediately to hand: three hide bags containing oddments of animal teeth and bones and scraps of hide. Off she sets to seek a new place to stay, but nobody will take her in, for all have heard of her disobedience to her father. So, finally finding herself alone on an isolated shore, she sits down and roots in the bags she has brought. Seizing a handful of teeth she scatters them upon the sand, and suddenly the beach is lined with seals and walruses. She throws bits of blubber into the sea and mighty whales appear; she strews the nearby tundra with bones and scraps of skin and it is suddenly full of grazing reindeer. All that is needed now, she thinks, are people to hunt and herd these various beasts, so she takes two small stones and calls them man and woman. Before she knows it a bustling community of men, women and children has sprung up – and to her amazement all address her respectfully as grandmother.

And, what is much more amazing still, her face, she suddenly finds, is old and wrinkled; the virgin girl now has the aspect of an ancient matriarch. Her work has aged her, ravaging her youthful beauty; for such is the cost to woman of her life-giving creativity.

31

Learning to Live

The world as first created was no fit place for animals or humans but a scene of darkness, savage anarchy and oppression. The Earth had to be adapted to the needs of its inhabitants who then had to learn to live harmoniously with nature.

In the early days, say the Tagish people, the Yukon was tyrannized by bloodthirsty giants, enormous wolverines, lynxes and other predators ravenous for the taste of flesh. Their rule, however, was to be challenged by Beaver, the resourceful trickster, who would eventually make the world safe for ordinary animals and people.

Setting off to do battle with the monsters, he first met a fierce-looking giant. Retreating before him, Beaver backed up a nearby mountain. But then, reaching the summit, he suddenly sprang at his persecutor, hanging on grimly as they rolled down the slope. When they got to the bottom, Beaver lay on top of the helpless giant and killed him by stabbing him in the hand – where all his strength lay. He then cut him into pieces, and scattered the scraps all about him in the forest. Each one became a harmless little rock rabbit.

Beaver-man and Mink-woman

Beaver's mission was by no means over, for there were many more tyrants to be checked and gentler species to be created. First he found Mink-woman smoking and tanning human skins by the river. Slinky and sinuous, she came close to seducing him – but he was wary of the wombful of writhing, spitting young he saw inside her. Bidding her close her eyes, he heated a sharp sliver of stone in the fire, before thrusting the deadly rock deep inside her. With a terrifying yell, she died and Beaver then called out to her young: they were no longer to be born as giant man-eating mink, he said, but more innocuous animals: mice, weasels, squirrels – and, of course, mink of the normal size.

Continuing on his way, Beaver met the wolverine, the eagle and other giant predators: he taught them all to remain as small as they were

This 20th-century Yupik beaver mask was used in ritual dances to celebrate Beaver-man whose bravery helped tame the wild world of old. The human face and extra pair of hands represent the beaver's *inua*, or human spirit.

The Origins of Fire and Death

Once the only flint in the world was owned by the bear. The other animals, however, conspired to steal a piece of it for themselves and enacted a cunning plan hatched by the mouse.

One day, the mouse asked the bear for some fur to make his young a nest. The bear saw nothing wrong in this, so he let the enterprising young father nose about in his fur. Suddenly he realized that the mouse had found the flint in its hiding place beneath his tail, and before he could act the wily rodent had thrown his loot to the waiting fox. Although the bear set off in pursuit he had no chance of catching the fox, who at once began breaking up the flint into fragments and distributing it among the other animals.

Buoyed up by his success, the fox went down to the lake. He broke the surface with a hollow reed and marvelled as water came seeping up through it. How wonderful it would be, he said, if when people were dead and buried they might rise again in this way. But the bear heard this comment, and he was in a dark mood. He hurled a rock into the water, interrupting the fox's reverie: as far as he was concerned, he roared, the dead could just lie there like lumps of stone. And so it has turned out: our lives have thankfully been transformed by fire, but when we come to die it is for ever.

at birth, and to settle for a diet of smaller animals, not people. He taught the sheep – until then a ferocious carnivore – to content himself with grass, and when the giant bear proved unwilling to take instruction he trapped and killed him. If the Yukon's animal predators had to learn their place, so too did its human hunters, like the man Beaver came upon cooking an otter he had killed. Although he welcomed the wayfarer courteously and invited him to share his meal, Beaver refused: he did not eat otter, he said, and nor should men – and he showed him how to cook and eat fish instead. So Beaver worked his way along the river, righting wrongs and restoring order, and in this way he cleaned up the entire Yukon valley.

Sharing for Stability

Although northern hunters have always had to kill animals to live, they have never seen nature as a rival to struggle against. Instinctive ecologists, they have always sensed the need for restraint, and respect for the animals they hunted. Man has much to learn from the animals, as is suggested by a Yukon tale of a boy taken into the river and educated by the fish. Other creatures are our equals and the resources of nature must be shared out fairly, so that all may co-exist in perfect balance. For it is in the stability of the system as a whole that the security of the single individual or group must lie: to seize more than one's share is ultimately to jeopardize one's own existence.

33

The Division of Night and Day

In every age and culture humanity has recognized the sun's importance as bringer of light and life, but in an Arctic scene sunk deep in darkness for long stretches of the year, the light shed by the sun is particularly treasured.

A myth from Siberia describes how a great elk once roamed the deep forests of the Earth. One day, he galloped out of the woods and up the slopes of a nearby mountain. Reaching the summit, he stood on his hind legs and reared heavenwards. With a single sweeping blow he dashed the sun from its place in the roof of the universe, then bore his blazing trophy back down the mountainside in triumph. Now the dark woods were filled with radiant sunlight. Where there had been an azure sky, in contrast, there was only blackness.

In the world of men, meanwhile, there was consternation at this terrible act of theft – and the great hero Main determined to put it right. He was a skilful hunter, accomplished and alert, and he sped off heavenwards to the upper Earth in pursuit of the elk. Following the light that blazed from the animal's dazzling crown he caught up with his quarry on the point of midnight. Main sent a swift arrow flying from his bow, brought down the elk and recovered the stolen sun.

Having restored it to its rightful place in the sky, this brave man was transformed into a spirit and entrusted with the task of guarding the sun for all time to come. Ever since he has had to maintain his unblinking vigilance, for every evening the elk has returned to snatch his charge away. Every night, accordingly, Main has had to hunt him down and kill him afresh, that the sun might be restored to the sky, and day once more break down below in the world of men.

Raven Steals Daylight

A major mythic strand, prevalent throughout northern Canada, Siberia and Alaska, recounts how Raven used his powers to bring light to the world. One typical tale tells how Raven stole daylight from a miser who kept it concealed at home.

One day Raven heard of a mean old man who had hoarded away a mysterious source of radiance which could transform the darkened universe. Tired of the incessant gloom, the heroic bird determined to claim this treasure and set off to find the man's ice-house. When he got there he sneaked into the entrance passage and peeked

With the Arctic year divided between two lengthy periods of darkness and light, it is no surprise that myths about the sun and moon abound in northerly regions. Here the sun sets over Echo Bay, close to the Arctic Circle in Canada's Northwest Territories.

into the living area. It was flooded with brilliant light coming from a ball covered with caribou hide, which was suspended from the centre of the ceiling. He was wondering how he was going to steal it when he heard the miser's young daughter talking – and Raven had an idea. Exerting all the force of his will he set to work on the mind of the little girl, and implanted in her a burning desire to play with the ball. The miser was reluctant but his daughter's resolve was stiffened by Raven's concentration. She begged and pleaded, and in time her tears wore down her father's resistance.

The child played delightedly with her toy, throwing it this way and that about the house, and soon it rolled out into the passage where Raven was waiting. He snatched it up in his beak and fled, desperately trying to tear it open as he flew. Raven struggled with the tightly sewn hide as a peregrine pursued him with venomous curses and threats. But just as it seemed to be upon him, Raven's feverish attempts to release the light paid

off: the ball's stitching finally split along the seam and its dazzling contents came spilling forth to illuminate the world. The peregrine at once yelled "Darkness!", and the world was returned to impenetrable gloom. But cool Raven merely shouted back "Light!", and the Earth was again flooded in daylight, for once out of the bag, this bright prize could never be put back. The two birds went on arguing together, alternating dark night and bright day – and so it has continued ever since, and always will.

Smiling at the Sun

After a long winter, Inuit would welcome the return of the sun from a high vantage point.

At the North Pole there are only a few months of daylight each year. Although conditions in the regions further south are rather less extreme, for much of the winter, noon will retain little more than a twilit glow from a sun which never quite manages to rise. And for all Arctic peoples there will be a few weeks or months each winter when daytime seems suspended and the community must sit out the enduring night until the light returns. Special spells were uttered for protection through this period, and when the sun rose triumphantly again, there was much joyful celebration. Throughout the Inuit lands, people would smile at the sun when it reappeared. But, mindful that winter was by no means over, they only smiled on one side of the face, keeping the other fixed resolutely straight.

The Bright and Lustful Moon

Further south, the sun is seen as guardian of the day, the moon a mere night-light to the sleeping world. But for much of the Arctic year the sun fails to rise and the land is bathed in a spectral light – giving the moon an importance unheard of in more southerly cultures.

A brother and a sister once shared a house, each the other's truest helpmate and most devoted friend. One night, however, when all the community slept, a stranger stole through the darkness and, forcing his way into the girl's bed, raped her, before slinking off again into the shadows. In her shock and shame the young woman said nothing about her ordeal, only wishing she could forget it and pretend it had never happened. That was a vain hope, however, for night after brutal night her assailant returned, to compound her humiliation.

Over time, however, her terror gave way to rage. Finding it unforgivable that her oppressor should go unpunished, she resolved to find out just who he was and then publicize his vileness before all his kinsfolk. She made her move on the night of the community's next big festival when, making her excuses early to the riotous company, she withdrew and made preparations to retire. Before lying down, she ran her thumb round the base of her cooking pot, blackening it with soot.

Not long after, her nocturnal visitor came to her bed again; she had no alternative but to submit once more to his coercion. But, focusing her mind on her plan, she ensured that this time her attacker left with a soot-marked nose.

Moments later she heard a roar of laughter which appeared to announce that he had returned to the feast and his absurd disfigurement had been noticed. The girl at once ran grim-faced to the public area to denounce him. Her horror and disbelief can only be imagined when she entered the communal hall to see the black smudge marking out the face of her beloved brother. Seizing a sharp knife, she cut off her breast before the astonished eyes of all, and held the bloody offering out before her, on a dish, to her persecutor. "If my body is so delectable to you," she asked, "why not eat this too?" Then, crazed with shame and grief, she stuck a clump of moss on the end of a sharp stick, soaked it in oil and set it alight, running out into the darkness with her impromptu torch.

Her brother ran after her, waving a brand of his own – though where his sister's had flared up bright and golden, his only smouldered sullenly. Their watching kinsfolk gaped incredulously as first the unhappy girl, then her brother, began to rise, revolving slowly, into the air. The sister is now the sun, her brother the silver moon, and their headlong chase has still not been concluded. For, just as the sun sinks over the eastern horizon the moon can be seen rising in the west; he goes circling after her, but can never quite catch up.

A mask of the Moon Spirit, from Alaska. While the mythologies of more southerly cultures often revered the sun, the peoples of the Arctic saw the moon as prime bringer of fertility and food.

An Absent Father

A woman, badly beaten by her husband, called out to the heavens in desperation. Moon was touched by her suffering and carried her off to his lunar home. When she fell pregnant by him, he gave her a special cooking pot and sent her back down to Earth.

Moon told her that she had to return home to bear the baby as her husband's own. As the consort of Moon, however, she should eat only that food which he himself provided. Whenever she placed her cooking pot on the fire it would be filled with delicious stew cooked by the moon-man himself. Then he restated the condition: on no account should she or her child eat the food her husband brought home.

The woman did as she was told, and the family prospered. Soon, however, her husband grew resentful. He spent many long days tracking beasts across the snow for their supper. He was the provider of the house, and now his role had been usurped. One day, hoping to appease him, the woman gave in to her husband's complaints and ate some of his food, giving some also to her child: by the very next morning, both had died.

Stone and ivory sculpture entitled *Mother and Child*, by Syolli Weekaluktuk, 1957.

There are several versions of this myth which account for a number of other celestial phenomena. One claims that the red that streaks the sky at dawn and sunset represents the blood of the sun-girl's severed breast, while sunspots are splashes of gore marking her radiant face. The dark patches on the moon are seen as the smudges of soot which still stain her brother's nose.

Every now and then, some Inuit say, he manages to get close enough to grab at his sister: then those on Earth see the sun partially obscured in lunar eclipse. A solar eclipse results, it is suggested, when she leaves the sky to come down to Earth to relieve her bowels or hunt for food. The moon, too, needs to eat: each month he can be seen waning, until his sister offers him her breast again which returns him to his former plumpness.

Variations of this same story are told from the far northeast of Siberia to eastern Greenland. All agree that the moon is male and the sun female, even though this reverses a view that is widespread throughout the rest of the world. The softness of the moon's light (and, for those cultures which were aware of it, the fact that it passively reflected the rays of the sun) have meant that for many ages and peoples the moon has been seen as the sun's feminine partner. In the Arctic, however, the difference in power between the two is much less evident. The sun may disappear for much of the year, and even at its zenith lack the scorching force it has in the latitudes to the south, but the moon of the Arctic winter can stay risen for days on end, its eerie half-light intensified by a bright reflective surface of ice and snow.

A Skyful of Stars

Often dazzlingly bright in winter, the stars still play an important role in Arctic mythology despite perpetual daylight through much of the summer. And many myths see them not as distant cosmic phenomena, but as decidedly intimate, human characters.

The myth of the moon-brother and his sun-sister, is also used to explain the creation of the stars, for when the brother saw that his torch glowed with a light much weaker than his sister's, he blew on it, sending a shower of sparks out into the air. His own light remained obstinately dim, but the sparks burned on brightly, spilling across the entire night sky as scattered stars.

Other Arctic peoples, however, suggest alternative origins. Among the Athapaskans of southern Alaska and the northwesternmost parts of subarctic Canada, the tale of the "Star Husbands" is told.

Two sisters, the story goes, had got well into adulthood without marrying; they were proud, self-satisfied women and none of the young men on offer around them met their exacting requirements. But one night as they slept they had the strangest dream: looking up at the heavens they saw two stars of surpassing beauty. Such was their charm that the women agreed they might make acceptable husbands. They then slept peacefully on. But they had a surprise in store the next morning – for each awoke in the embrace of a fine and handsome young man.

The astonished women asked the men what they thought they were doing in their beds. The men then reminded the women how the previous night they had longed for the two stars as their husbands. Now their own heartfelt wish had been granted: they were high up in the heavens with the partners of their choice. When the sisters asked what had become of their families, the stars replied that they had left them behind in the world of mortals and that they should resign themselves to never seeing them again. The sisters wept and tore at their garments, but in vain: for this was their life now and they had to accept its rules.

The stars, however, could not remain untouched by their grief and they did all they could for their earthly in-laws, stealing down by night to leave offerings of food and fur outside their home. The parents were grateful and so too were the girls. Yet they missed their mortal kin so much their thoughts turned increasingly to escape.

One day when their husbands were out hunting, the sisters pleated together a string of pelts, and slid down it back to Earth. Their parents were overjoyed to have their daughters back; the sisters relieved to be restored to an earthly community they would never again make the mistake of undervaluing. Their husbands, on the other hand, were desolate at their loss: night after night they came to their wives in their dreams, imploring them to return. In time, though, they accepted that mortal women needed their mortal kin around them. Selfless in their affections, they went on helping out the sisters and their family with food, fur and other favours – and even when, having learned their lesson the hard way, the sisters finally condescended to marry Athapaskan men, their star husbands bore them no resentment. Magnanimous to the last, they watched over the whole community, keeping it from all scarcity and harm.

The Silver Maid of the Saami

Specific stars and constellations also have their own origin myths. Sirius, for instance, which is characterized by continually flickering colour-changes, is said by certain Inuit people to be the soapstone lamp of an ill-tempered celestial crone. She is pictured sitting by the window of her ice-house, nursing its flame, and muttering angrily to herself every time a passer-by disturbs it with another draught. But the account the Saami of Arctic Scandinavia offer for the formation of the Milky Way is a more romantic story altogether.

They tell the tale of the Silver Maid, a beautiful, but bashful, young virgin with whom all the district's young men were besotted. She refused them all, though, and was so fleet of foot that none of them could catch her. One youth, however, resolved to win her or die in the attempt and for a time it seemed he might succeed. Forcing her to flee up a mountainside he appeared to have her trapped at the top when, laughing, she stepped into the air and ran off into the clouds.

Defeated in what had seemed to be his moment of triumph, the young man collapsed, and appeared to be on the point of death. Seeing the terrible damage her proud chastity had done, the distraught girl returned to his side, bitterly regretting her reckless playfulness. In the desperate hope of reviving him, she squeezed milk from her virgin breast, but an unforgiving wind dashed the drops from his dying lips, scattering them far and wide across the endless heavens. Some of the milk was blown back upon its giver, freezing her into a silver statue.

Thus was created the perfect memorial to a woman whose compassion had not matched her beauty. The Silver Maid was entrancing in appearance, but cold and hard to the touch. Her one moment of tenderness was commemorated, however, in that Milky Way which splashes with such abundance across the sky.

Yupik masks representing the sun, moon and stars with the wind suggested by the small feathers in the mouths, c.19th century.

Holes in Heaven

It is not only stars that emanate from far spirit planes, for the Inuit believe that the elements too descend from distant realms above.

Given their belief that this world is but one of several realms of existence, stacked one on top of another, the Inuit see the sky as the floor of Heaven. Above, some say, is another world just like our own, but peopled with the living spirits of the mortal dead, who while away a blissful eternity hunting game or playing football.

The stars they see as holes in the hard vault of the heavens: through them the souls of the deceased make their ascent to everlasting happiness in a rich green country watered by lakes and running streams. Often when these torrents are in full spate, water spills through the holes of the upper Earth, to fall as snow or summer rain on the realms beneath. Here the sun shines brightly all year; there is always light and it too seeps through the star-holes, creating what we see as celestial radiance.

The Spirit of the Wind

Living close to the elements, Arctic-dwellers are prey to the force of the billowing wind. But the blustering squall which blows across the open ground is not seen as a cruel foe: for it is the breath of the living world, the animating spirit of a cold and hostile land.

In milder climates, the weather can be taken for granted because only freak extremes will endanger the community. In the Arctic, however, extremity is the norm and sudden changes in weather conditions can spell disaster. Here nothing can be done without the consent of the elements.

It is no wonder then that Sila, the Inuit spirit of the wind and weather, should have proved so influential. Identified equally with the icy gale and with the softer breath by which humans and animals live, Sila is that vital spirit which enlivens the whole world. As changeable as the wind itself, he manifests himself in all manner of different forms: not just in violent storms but in stillness and calm; not only in the unpredictability of the weather but in the lively intelligence of humankind.

Proud Lord of the Winds

The Nenets of Siberia talk of Kotura, Lord of the Winds. One story they tell about him describes how their encampment had been battered for weeks on end by an apparently endless blizzard. Eventually a Nenets elder sent his eldest daughter off into the snows to plead with Kotura for respite. The girl made her way safely to Kotura's tent and, finding it empty, simply helped herself to food. The returning giant looked askance, but said nothing, just asking her to take some food to his elderly neighbour. Outside, the blizzard seemed angrier than ever and the girl decided to abandon her errand. At a short distance from Kotura's tent she dumped the food and headed back. When he asked her what the old woman had given her in return she replied, "Nothing". Kotura was suspicious, but remained silent.

Next morning, however, before he went out hunting, he left the girl an untreated reindeer hide. By nightfall, he said, he expected her to have made him a coat, shoes and mittens. The girl started work, but with neither the time nor the tools to do the job properly, she struggled. When a withered old crone called at the door mid-morning to ask her to help her get some dust out of her eye, the girl angrily sent her packing, complaining that she had no time to spare. Eventually, she did manage to patch together a coat, shoes and mittens of sorts by the end of the day. But the job was botched, and Kotura reacted angrily, taking her by the leg and flinging her far off into the snow to die.

As the weeks went by, there was still no let-up in the weather, so the old man sent out his second daughter. She, however, fared no better, and back at the Nenets camp the storm raged on.

Now it was up to the third and favourite daughter. She was an obliging and amiable girl. On finding Kotura's tent she waited politely to be asked in to eat; sent with food for his neighbour, she would not rest till she had delivered it through the blizzard. In gratitude the old woman gave her two sharp knives, some bone needles and scrapers. Bemused, she took them back to the giant, who smiled, but said nothing.

Alaskan reindeer and sealskin boots, decorated with caribou hide, dyed dog hair, wolverine fur and coloured thread.

The Tempest Tamed

Arctic-dwellers do not believe they are completely helpless before the elements, as this story of an enterprising young Thompson River Indian boy suggests.

In subarctic Manitoba they say that the wind once terrorized the world unchecked. No tree was safe and no tent could be raised. In fact, no human activity was possible when the wind did not wish it and the Indians accepted the tyranny of the storm since they had not known any other way. But one little boy thought otherwise and he determined to domesticate the wind.

The proud youth carefully set a series of snares out where the land was most exposed. The wind screamed derisively for days until, to its astonishment, it found it was well and truly trapped. It bucked and howled in its efforts to escape, but the boy quickly gathered it up into a blanket, and carried it off in triumph to show to his people. When he told them of his success they laughed scornfully, refusing to believe his story. But they gasped in amazement when he loosened a corner of his blanket and the wind came rushing out.

Bundling it back into its place, the boy agreed to release it only on condition that it quieten down. But the wind insisted that sometimes it

would be obliged to blow up a storm, but when that happened it would turn the dawn sky red to give them advance warning.

Next morning, however, the giant set her the same task that had defeated her sisters – and the tools came into their own. Even so, she was wondering how she would complete the job on time when the old woman called at the door with something in her eye. Rushed as she was, the girl broke off to assist her, whereupon four women leaped out of the old woman's ear and set about helping with the hide. In no time the job was done: coat, hat and mittens, all beautifully made.

When the giant returned, he was full of admiration. Not only did he love her himself, he said, but his mother and four sisters loved her too: all wanted her to stay with him and be his bride. With those words, the storm suddenly stilled and, far away across the tundra, the old man knew his youngest daughter had saved her people. Great rejoicing was there that day: not only for the ceasing of the storm, but for the fortune of a brave and generous young woman.

Magical Souls of Light

The awesome lightshows that splash a haunting glow across the Arctic sky are famed today as the Aurora Borealis, or Northern Lights. For generations of Inuit, however, this dramatic spectacle has provided one of their most colourful myths.

Illuminating the winter darkness with spectral flashes of green light, the Aurora Borealis is one of the most sublime sights this Earth has to offer. But where explorers from southern lands have seen a wondrous play of light, the Inuit have found in its fluctuations a very different kind of game.

Across the Arctic region people have explained the phenomenon of the Aurora Borealis in substantially the same way: that the changing shades of luminescence represent the souls of departed children who are playing football. In those shifting, shimmering forms can be sensed the figures of these spirit sportsmen, kicking a walrus skull around between them, caught up completely in their enduring game.

The Aurora Borealis is more than just a visual phenomenon, however – for beneath the nimble feet of these ghostly footballers, the air can be heard crackling. To the Inuit these distant sounds are like running footsteps on a delicate crust of snow. And, furthermore, just as the listeners can discern the movements of these ethereal sportsmen, so can they in turn hear the sounds made by the mortals who watch them: whistle, say the Inuit, and these dead souls will draw nearer.

Elsewhere in the Arctic there are other explanations for the Aurora. The Saami of northern Scandinavia regard it as a single entity and characterize it as another heavenly personage, like the sun and moon. Unlike the Inuit, the Saami see the moon as feminine and the sun as masculine and

for them the Aurora is also male – a nocturnal rival to the daytime sun. According to them, when Sun started looking about him to find a fit bride for Peivalke, his beloved son, his first thought was to ask Moon for the hand of her beautiful daughter. That was impossible, Moon replied, because the girl was only a baby, far too young and delicate to wed. Peivalke's blazing body would scorch her skin, she continued. And besides, she was already promised to Nainas, leader of the mighty Northern Lights.

Piqued to be thus slighted, Sun shook the skies with thunder and lashed the Earth with rain and hailstorms, while his roaring winds churned up the seas. Taking refuge in darkness, Moon wondered how her daughter might best be concealed. Eventually she saw an elderly couple living on a little island in the middle of a lake. There, surely, she would be safe, and so she left her where the old man and woman might find her. They were overjoyed that such an appealing waif had come their way. Niekia, they named her, and she grew up the most beautiful young woman imaginable, only a certain pallor providing any hint of unearthly origins.

An Inuit bear-skin ball. The football players that many Arctic-dwellers saw in the Aurora Borealis were, to a great extent, reflections of themselves since such games were very popular throughout the region.

Even in this seclusion, such a secret could not be kept for long, and in time Sun himself heard of Niekia's beauty. He sent Peivalke to find her and he fell in love with her at first sight. She, however, could not endure the searing heat of the young Sun's love, and she melted away before his anguished eyes. Wandering off across the icy tundra, she came by daybreak to the ocean shore and there, in an isolated hut, she slept out the day. She was woken at nightfall by the sound of armed men arriving. They were the handsome warriors known as the Northern Lights, led by the bold Nainas.

Love in a Magical Light

Having feasted, the boisterous troop of soldiers performed a ferocious sword-dance before retiring for the night. But Nainas stayed behind, sensing the presence of the mysterious woman – and in the nocturnal silence he called her quietly to him. In a moment Niekia emerged from the darkness and the young couple fell into each other's arms. They knew, there and then, that they were destined for one another. And so indeed it seemed.

For a time they lived together in every happiness – except that Niekia found her husband's day-long absences so hard to bear. He solemnly explained that he had to go to war, with his great rival with whom he struggled for the rule of the skies: if he stayed after daybreak, he would be an easy target for the rising Sun.

Niekia heard his words, but could not find it in her heart to accept what her husband said: she racked her brains for a way to keep him with her through the day. At last she hit upon an idea: making a quilt of reindeer hide, she embroidered it with all the stars and constellations of the night, then hung it across the ceiling of her hut. When Nainas began to stir at the dawn of day, he opened his bleary eyes and saw what appeared to be the night sky overhead. Reassured, he turned over and went back to sleep. But when, hugging herself in triumph, Niekia walked out of her hut into the brightness of day, the open door let sunbeams steal in to where Nainas lay. Blinking awake, he realized what had happened, called his warriors and rushed out for the fray. But he had risen too late, and Sun caught him on the open ground in the broadest daylight. He sent a burning shaft of light hurtling down at his old enemy, but Niekia managed to shield her husband from its impact, and he succeeded in struggling clear and flying away. The furious Sun seized Niekia and swore that she would at least now have to marry his son. When she defied him to do his worst, declaring she would never comply, he became enraged and hurled her into the arms of her watching mother. And her dark shadow can be seen draped across the Moon's dazzling form to this very day.

The vaulting skies that rise above the Arctic lands have had a profound influence on the northern imagination. The haunting glow of the Aurora Borealis, seen here from Churchill, Manitoba, in northern Canada, is just one of the reasons why.

An Ever-Changing Land

For Arctic-dwellers the landscape is a living entity. Not only does it feed and nurture countless beasts and people but its very substance seems permeated with vital energy, its every contour animated by the associations of myth and memory.

Battling against the wind high above the limitless expanse of water, Raven scanned the sea with mounting dismay. He had braved many dangers to release light into the universe and now he searched in vain for somewhere to rest his weary body. But just as he was beginning to despair, the waters seemed to swell and sputter beneath him, and a dark form suddenly broke the surface of the sea: a mighty sea beast, its vast body extending from one horizon to the other. Thrusting its great frame into the air to breathe, it promptly plunged back beneath the waves, its giant tail-flukes smashing the surface as it dived.

This typical Arctic scene, of College Fjord in Alaska, shows how the forces of nature have conspired over time to change the ancient landscape. Here icebergs, snowdrifts and swirling winds are continually altering the face of the land.

The great whale vanished far beneath the waves, but Raven remained watchful for he knew that sooner or later the beast would have to come up for air again: and this time he would be ready. Sure enough, the whale's vast bulk could soon be seen rushing upwards to the ocean's surface. Harpoon in his hand, Raven waited and sent his weapon whistling through the air. Striking the monster's massive head, the line snapped taut and so began a long, hard struggle between the two. One moment the whale seemed defeated, the next Raven floundered as his colossal catch thrashed violently about, threatening to drag him headlong down into the depths. But Raven sensed a growing slackness in the line, and finally the whale floated listlessly to the surface, its life's breath ebbing. Dead at last, it lay still in the water, its vast outline rising high above the lapping waves. Here was land, thought Raven; here men might live out a worthwhile existence.

Thus the Inuit of Tikigaq, on the northern coast of Alaska, explain the creation of their land. Not only does the myth account for the distinctive hump-backed shape of the peninsula they inhabit but it commemorates the whale-hunt which for centuries has been central to their way of life.

That their homeland should once have surged through the sea, a living whale, seems entirely appropriate. While it has endured millennia, the Arctic landscape may at the same time change from minute to minute, recreated endlessly by the Arctic weather. Drifting snow subtly reshapes the contours of the country day by day; avalanches tear away whole hillsides at a moment's notice. Pack ice creeps outwards from the coast, blurring the boundary between land and sea, just as blizzards white out the frontier between Earth and sky. Year in, year out, the ice expands and contracts, slightly different in extent and consistency each season, while, crashing free to launch themselves at intervals from the inching glaciers that bred them, the newly created icebergs come and go. The Inuit looking out upon their homeland are observing no static scene, but a vast living, breathing, ever-changing creature.

Across the Arctic region, objects such as this Koryak sculpture were offered up at special festivals to ensure the spirit of the whale was renewed and thus help future generations thrive.

Landscape as Memory

If the Arctic landscape is possessed of such an elemental life-force, it also resonates with the myriad associations of myth and memory. For every aspect of life and culture is reflected in the environment: every feature has its appointed place in the human scheme. Arctic-dwellers know each mountain, each promontory or inlet by its own name. Here, this place-name announces, fine walrus may be found; there, the appelation proclaims, a man may hunt spotted seal. Kayaks can make their way up here, the name of one stream suggests; there, another warns, they are best carried.

Thus enshrined in the Arctic landscape are multifarious clues as to its effective use, but the scene also serves as an anthology of stories. Those conical hills on the horizon have reminded untold generations of a woman's breasts, for instance; that jagged outcrop is reminiscent of a harpoon head. Every such feature offers a glancing allusion to a story of the region, a reminder of the mythic history of the land and its inhabitants. That depression marks the spot where Raven pecked the earth to bring the land into being; those hummocks are the ice-houses of the giants who sought to stop him. Knowing their own native region as a "memoryscape", Arctic-dwellers orientate themselves both geographically and psychologically. And once the features of their locality are marked in their minds from childhood on, they are able to "think" their way around their homeland in even the most appalling weather conditions.

45

In Search of the Elements

The food and clothing that animals provided were essential to Arctic peoples. They were of little use, however, without fire and fresh water. These two elements were vital for life in the frigid north, as a tale told by the Thompson River Indians illustrates.

Although the homeland of the Thompson River Indians is dotted with lakes and criss-crossed with rivers, for much of the year water is at a premium. Only "dry", deep-frozen snow falls during the winter months, while surface water is locked up by the cold, every lake is ice-hard and every stream at a standstill. Fortunately the Indians have fire, and can thaw out whatever water they require – but without fire there would be no water and that would make life intolerably harsh indeed.

Yet that is precisely how things stood in the first days of the world. Then it seems the people sipped what moisture they could from the morning dew, and relied for food on raw birds' eggs, berries, roots and leaves. On this diet, the summers passed agreeably enough: the winters, though, were another matter entirely. With no fire to call upon, the people had to huddle together for warmth in underground lodges, while cooking, of course, was completely out of the question. There was no way of eating meat, therefore, nor any way of melting out sufficient drinking quantities of ice water. The people thus had a meagre time of it, subsisting on what they had managed to scrimp and save from the previous summer. Many, inevitably, succumbed to starvation; those who survived did so only in the most abject wretchedness, their life a curse of yearning and horror.

This was no way to live, by any decent standards, and yet the Indians knew no better, never imagining that a different sort of existence might be possible. Still less did it occur to them that they might hold the solution in their own hands. So it was to prove, however.

A certain elder of the community lived in a dugout lodge with his young son. Although supposedly a shaman, he accepted his people's destiny as passively as they did, never guessing at the true extent of the powers he possessed. Not once, for instance, did he think of opening either of the two wooden chests which stood in a corner of his own lodge, and which had done, similarly unopened, for generations. He took it for granted that what was not already known could only be harmful: it would be asking for trouble to pry.

The chests were works of the utmost beauty. Each was richly carved with animals, trees and flowers, and both had a special symbol etched upon the lid. On the first was a shining sun, its brightness radiating out upon the world beneath; on the other a set of wavy lines suggested a sensuous flowing river. His son often wondered what

A birchbark box made by the Nivkhi people from Siberia.
The spirals represent the cosmic serpent, creator of the universe.

they contained but, mindful of his father's warning, he never dreamed of opening either box.

Some spirit seems to have taken pity on the people, however, for one day a stranger came to call at the lodge while the father was out hunting, and only his son was home. The gentleman at once turned to the chests and began asking questions about them. This piqued the boy's own curiosity but, ever the faithful son, he remained dogged in what he saw as his duty. So when the mysterious visitor asked him to open one of the boxes he steadfastly refused. He resisted all the stranger's hints and insinuations, so eventually his visitor resorted to plain trickery. He asked the boy to check if his father was coming home, and the boy went out to look. Waiting until his back was turned, the man went over to the first chest and, with a quick look over his shoulder, threw open the lid. The chest seemed to contain immeasurable depths and deep down inside it, a strange bubbling sound was heard. Moments later water came gushing forth in a rushing torrent. Welling up from the underground lodge it poured out into the world, quickly filling up the rivers, streams and lakes: from now on, the people would never run out of water.

The boy looked on dumbfounded as his visitor then opened the second chest; he shrank back in alarm as flames shot forth from its depths. Searing the roof clean off the lodge, the fire spread quickly through the adjacent trees, until soon the whole northern forest was burning brightly. Magical fire, it did not destroy the trees, instead touching each with its special spirit: from now on all would have the capacity to burn on man's behalf. No more need humanity fear the winter's rigours. Henceforth they would have fire and water to lend dignity to their life and labours.

Fire, greatest friend of man, the preparer of his food and heater of his home, was often seen as a central symbol of man's social existence. More

Ornamental stone lamps, such as this one from Kodiak Island, Alaska, burned oil from whales or other sea mammals to provide light and heat. Once lit, this one would also have cast shadows on the bear's head as it seemed to rise above the oil.

than this, though, bursting forth from a struck flint or a rubbed twig, crackling and prancing in a glowing hearth, it seemed to stand in its animation for life itself – hence its place in Inuit legend at humanity's beating heart.

This view of fire is reflected in one variant of the Tikigaq story of "Raven and the Whale" (see pages 44–45). Here, searching the primeval sea in search of a place to land, Raven once again came across a mighty whale. In this version of the tale, however, instead of harpooning it from a great height, he flew straight through the cold wind and down into its spreading jaws. In its dark interior he found a warm, welcoming and brightly illuminated ice-house. Seated before it, a beautiful woman carefully tended a lamp to keep alive its delicate flame. From time to time she vanished, to reappear again moments later. Asked why she was so restless, the woman replied that she was the whale's soul, and that she passed in and out of its blow hole with its every breath. The flame she tended so carefully was its living heart, so strong and vital and yet so fragile. One puff, and it would be extinguished as though it had never been.

The Shaman and the Smith

The cultures of Siberia had ancient contacts with the metalworking civilizations of China and Central Asia. The smith's ability to master fire and transform metal from one shape to another was closely linked to the shaman's powers of self-transformation.

One day towards the end of the nineteenth century, a Siberian boy fell sick with smallpox. In itself this was an unexceptional occurrence. What made this particular case so momentous, however, was that its victim was destined to find renown as Dyukhade, the great shaman of the Nganasan.

He would later recall the disease and its delirium as the road by which he descended to the underworld. A stoat and a mouse were his guides on this journey to understanding and power – and at the centre of his quest was his dismemberment and re-creation in the workshop of a blacksmith.

For seven days, said Dyukhade, his way was barred by seven cliffs, but finally he spied an opening and crept cautiously through. Blinking in the overwhelming glare of an infernal fire, he found himself in what he realized was some mighty forge. A cauldron half the size of the Earth hung over the roaring flames, urged on to ever-greater intensity by a naked blacksmith who worked steadily away with hide-covered bellows. Seeing the new arrival the craftsman reached out to the bench beside him for a pair of tongs: their grips were the size of tents and they all but crushed the life out of the dreaming Dyukhade. He was too paralyzed with fear to struggle against his fate, so he merely looked on helplessly as his body was systematically dismantled. First beheading him, the blacksmith sliced up the boy's body into small pieces which he boiled up in the cauldron for three whole years.

Only when every shred of flesh had been peeled away from every inch of bone did the smith see fit to remove what little remained.

The boy's head, meanwhile, he worked like so much metal, heating it until it glowed dull red then beating it upon a clanking anvil. With great swings of his arm, he smote the lump until sparks came showering down, filling the forge with flickering light and shadows. At intervals he tempered the iron by plunging it into ice-cold water, before removing it to heat and hammer again.

When he was satisfied that his work was done, the blacksmith reunited Dyukhade's head with his boiled bones, clothing them with flesh so that the boy regained his original appearance. Before returning him to the world, however, he took Dyukhade's skull and pierced the ears with his iron finger: henceforth he would understand the speech of healing herbs and plants.

According to a Sakha (Yakut) proverb, "Smiths and shamans come from the same nest," a view shared by all the peoples of Arctic Siberia. Many civilizations may have found magical properties in the blacksmith's craft, and Siberian peoples connected the two directly – for the smith's mastery of fire made him ritually superior to the shaman while he could also fashion those metal charms with which the shaman festooned his cloak as a magic armour against malevolent spirits. And if the smith could make iron as protection against malign influences, so too could he remake the very shamans themselves.

Koryak knife from Kamchatka, with whalebone handle and seal-hide sheath. Metalworking itself was imported to the region, as was the design which bears a Chinese influence.

Mistress of the Fire

Fire was an element which demanded the utmost respect. The Selkups of northern Siberia tell the tale of a young mother who treated her hearth with disdain, and paid a terrible price.

One evening the mother was rocking her baby by a fire when a spark shot out and caught the infant, who screamed in pain. The woman started cursing the fire and, laying her baby down, she took an axe and beat at the burning logs. Then she doused the embers with water until no trace of the fire was left: it served it right, she said, for hurting her child.

But now her tent was dark and cold. Unable to relight her fire, she went to ask her kinsfolk for some, but in each tent she called at the fire flickered and went out. Soon the whole camp was left in cold and darkness.

Everyone was angry with the young mother but one old woman agreed to come to her tent to find out how she had offended the Mistress of Fire. She rubbed sticks together with little success, but from the faint glow she did manage to create, the voice of the Fire Mistress could just be heard. The whole of humankind, she said, would now be deprived of fire because of this young woman's disrespect. She would only change her mind if the woman paid for her sacrilege with her own son. From his dying heart would be kindled the flame that would save humanity. Weeping, the mother handed over her beloved baby. The Mistress of Fire rose up in a towering flame and swept the infant up into the sky – and neither were ever seen again.

The young mother wept bitterly for her baby but in the camp and throughout the world beyond, men and women sighed with relief when all their fires came spluttering to life again.

THE SOUL OF THE WILD

Farming could not have originated in the Arctic latitudes, since for most of the year the earth was frozen as hard as any ploughshare and the landscape, when not deep in drifting snow, was scoured by hostile, icy winds. Darkness descended on the region for interminable weeks and months, snuffing out any struggling plant life, which needed the precious sunlight to breathe and grow. And when the summer finally came after the long haul of an icebound winter, it did so as a desperate, headlong sprint of life and death. A few fleeting weeks of thaw had to suffice for the tundra vegetation to complete entire regenerative cycles, plants springing up in a blaze of colour just long enough to flower, scatter seeds or spores, and replenish themselves, before hunkering down once more to endure the renewed onslaught of autumn ice and snow.

Until a few thousand years ago, no human had ever ploughed a furrow or planted a seed. Humankind lived by hunting and gathering. Once developed, agriculture spread through most of the southern landscape, but in the Arctic there remained no alternative except to eat fish and game. Animals have movement and will, just like humans, and for the hunter there was the constant uncertainty of whether or not they would allow themselves to be caught. The daily routines of Arctic hunters thus preserved the intricate subtleties of understanding nature and the animal world.

The image conjured by "man the hunter" projected a sense of masterful pride, but the reality was quite different. The poorest peasant farmer, scratching the most meagre living, was nonetheless taming the earth and bending nature to his will. The northern hunter, however, was never able to forget that he was taking only what the earth chose to allow him. The myths of the Arctic region reflected, therefore, a very different relationship between humanity and nature than was to be found in the mythologies of more southerly civilizations. Respect was the living heart of this relationship, and the hunter, while he may have taken its outer body, never subjugated his quarry. Dependent upon animals for all his food and clothing, he had to seek the acceptance and friendship of the creatures he aimed to kill. He needed them in a way that they would never need him. No human co-existed more closely with nature, paradoxically, than the hunter who killed animals so that he might live.

Opposite: **Yupik "black fish" mask of the many-toothed *qaculluut,* or wolf-fish. Hunters would make sure they appeased an animal's spirit before they hunted it down.**

Below: **The tools the Inuit used to hunt, like this whalebone walrus harpoon head, were often decorated with potent symbols, a sign of the hunter's respect for the hunted.**

51

The Hunter's Contract

In the Arctic world humans were completely dependent on animals to stay alive. Yet they had no given right to the bounty of nature; only by the willing consent of his quarry was the hunter ever successful – a consent which would be withheld if not fully earned.

For the hunters of the north there was no clear boundary between "humankind" and "nature". The Arctic environment was much too harsh for its human inhabitants to dream of mastery, for other creatures often had the edge when it came to survival. No man could claim to have the strength of the white bear, the awesome bulk of the whale or the tough resilience of the reindeer. If anything, animals seemed more dominant than the puny, helpless humans. Hence the widespread view that in the days of the first creation the animals were man-eaters, and that they slipped back and forth at will between their

animal and quasi-human forms. The Tagish Indians' tale of Beaver and his battles with the man-eaters (see page 32) suggested that even the most innocuous of creatures might have a stronger and more sinister side which those who preyed off them forgot at their peril.

Humankind's relative powerlessness was clear at the economic level too, surrounded as the hunters were by some of the animal kingdom's toughest survivors. Without the sinew-sewn furs and skins he stripped from other animals, a man would have frozen to death; without the flesh of the mammals and fish he killed he would quickly have starved. He could not have hunted were it not for his spearhead and harpoon of fashioned bone, while without whale oil he would have lived in darkness through long stretches of the year.

Many more southerly civilizations were reliant upon animals too, of course, but none as exclusively as these hunters of the north. For the hunter-gatherers of warmer climates meat was supplemented by myriad forms of plant food. Their dependence on the animal world was therefore never absolute. The nomadic herdsmen of the Asian steppes may have eaten, drunk and dressed in the produce of their livestock, but their flocks were semi-domesticated. The Arctic hunter, by contrast, had to go out and attempt to catch a quarry which had an independent will of its own. Even the most experienced and accomplished hunter was thus never in full control. He could stand stock-still for many hours beside a breathing

Animals permeated all aspects of life in the Arctic for they provided everything from food and tools to clothes and footwear, such as these 19th-century caribou-skin shoes.

hole and not see the seal whose movements he had been anticipating. He might trek for days in search of caribou and return empty-handed – or he could be lucky, and win a month's meat for his community with a few minutes' work. The hunter thus has to live with a level of uncertainty which no farmer could contemplate, and he does this by fine-tuning his sensitivities to animals and the environment in which they move.

Faced with the vagaries of a life in which the survival of whole families could depend on skill at finding sufficient game, hunters saw their relation to animals in terms of respect and careful negotiation. Throughout the Arctic the idea could be found that hunted animals consented to the kill, giving themselves up willingly to the hunter who had made them the appropriate offerings. The hunter had to earn his right to his prey by uttering prayers of praise and flattery; he was careful to give all due thanks for his success and deal respectfully with the carcass. He had to share his good fortune fairly with the other members of his community – otherwise he would find himself hunting fruitlessly next time.

The hunter's wife also had her part to play: she too had to show respect and gratitude for what her husband had caught, taking care in its cooking, and using its skin wisely and neatly when sewing (see pages 72–73). An elaborate system of taboos and obligations thus governed the relationship between killer and killed. In innumerable little acts of respect the hunter affirmed his awareness that he was taking the life of his spiritual equal, in keeping with what the Algonquins of northwestern Canada called the "Old Agreement".

Seal-gut was often used for raincoats and to cover windows. This 19th-century piece, however, has been decorated with male and female figures and an *umiaq*, a boat frequently used by families.

By the terms of this ancient understanding, men were allowed to hunt and kill what animals, birds and fish they needed and were given full use of their bodies – on the strict condition that they respected the living souls within.

For the bodies of animals, like those of people, were merely temporary clothing for immortal souls. (This notion was especially vivid for peoples accustomed to dressing in animal hides.) Not just animals and plants, in fact, but even mountains and snowstorms had what the Inuit call *inua*, or in-dwelling beings. The word comes from the same root as "Inuit" – "man" or "inhabitant" – itself, a mark of the continuity this people saw between man and nature. No superiority set the soul of the human apart, though the animals might take pity on man's physical weakness, yielding up their bodies to nourish and protect him in an environment in which he could not otherwise hope to survive. And just as humans reincarnated their ancestors from one generation to another (see pages 118–119), so slaughtered animals kept returning to clothe and feed them. Every time a hunter killed to eat, he took a life belonging to another soul, his equal – yet such was the generosity of these spirits that they submitted willingly to be killed over and over again through the generations. The least man could do in return was show gratitude for the animals' bounty: were he ever to shirk that duty, he would not find the animals so obliging.

53

Spirits of the Sea

Sea mammals provided many essential resources for the hunters of the Arctic, who had to wait patiently for them to appear at the water's surface before making their move. A complex code of conduct grew up to govern their exploitation.

A dark slash interrupting the white infinity of the ice-floe, the seal-hunter was visible from afar. Motionless he waited, harpoon poised for the strike – at the ready, and yet perfectly relaxed. He had been there hours already, and knew he might well remain for many more, yet it did not occur to him to feel frustrated. The seal-spirit was sure to sacrifice its life and no hunter could therefore begrudge his time. Crooning quietly, he offered up his patience to his intended quarry, along with praises for its beauty and intelligence.

Several hours later the slush was momentarily disturbed by the bubble that signalled exhaling below. A moment's inattention and the hunter would have missed it, but his gaze had been steady, his concentration complete: one downward thrust and the barbed harpoon-head struck savagely home. The hunter's yell of triumph echoed far out over the ice as the harpoon shaft spun harmlessly off to one side. The cord whipped through his mittened hands as the seal dived for safety, only to be pulled up short as the hunter hauled at his bucking catch. Meanwhile, the empty ice-floe filled up as his kinsfolk ran out in answer to his cry. The girls and women began to cry out in a long-drawn-out chorus of appreciation as the

hunter's wife crouched respectfully beside the dying seal. Melting snow in her cupped hand, she gave it a symbolic drink – just as an attentive hostess might to an honoured guest. Then, thanking it for condescending to be killed and apologizing for any pain, she opened its belly with a single stroke of her sharp knife.

The suspense of the breathing-hole vigil or the high drama of the ocean whale-hunt were the climax of months of preparation. Pre-Christianity, hunting for sea mammals was a quasi-religious ritual activity, to which these final confrontations between man and animal became almost incidental. Before the hunter could even consider embarking on an expedition, his wife had to ask the moon for his success. How she dealt with the carcass afterwards was also of incalculable importance. First she had to pour an offering of blood next to the victim's head in thanksgiving. Then, in the hope of further bounty in the future, she tore out the kidneys and tossed them aside on the ice. "May there be more where this came from," she would say. These courtesies observed, the kill could then be butchered, but there were still strict protocols to be followed. The body had to be cut up neatly and the meat and blubber shared equally around: the

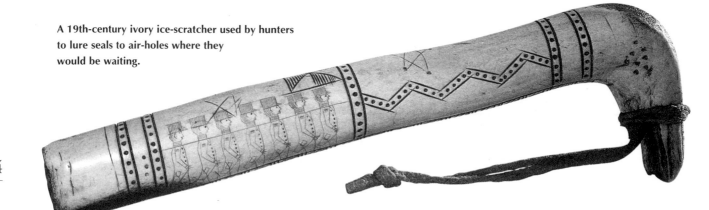

A 19th-century ivory ice-scratcher used by hunters to lure seals to air-holes where they would be waiting.

animal was its own creature, not the property of any individual or single household. The hide had to be skilfully fashioned to make a "second skin" for its human wearer – no creature wanted to sacrifice itself for the sake of some sloppy sewing. People said it was not the harpoon but a woman's needle which made the successful hunter. Even the state of the meat store was important: it had to be clean, fresh and inviting.

A Woman and a Whale

According to the Alaskan Inupiat: "The whale comes to the whaler's wife, not to the whaler." Throughout the whaling season, the womenfolk had to stay at home thinking peaceful thoughts, moving slowly and calmly, keeping cares at bay and acting generously. A woman's restfulness, it was thought, would set the whale at ease as her quiet soul called out welcomingly to his.

The intimacy of the bond between woman and whale is hinted at a tale told by the hunters of coastal Siberia.

A lonely young woman, neglected by her husband, was given to walking in solitude along the ocean strand. One early morning, to her astonishment, a whale emerged from the waves and rode up on to the beach: from its open mouth stepped the most handsome man she had ever seen. Through succeeding nights their friendship developed, their feelings growing ever fonder. For the first time the woman felt appreciated and loved. But her idyll was not to last: one night her jealous husband followed her and discovered his rival. In a fury, he chased the whale-man down to the water's edge where he struggled into his whaleskin to make his escape. He was not quick enough, however: the husband's harpoon caught him full in the flank. Blood gushed forth as the whale slipped back beneath the waves and swam disconsolately out to sea. The whale-man was never seen again, but in time his lover gave birth to a little whale. At first she kept him in a bucket; then in a small hollow, which can still be seen in her village today. Soon, though, she had to turn

The First Seal

When a hunter made his first kill a bond was sealed between him and his prey to ensure such success continued in the future.

When a young Inuit boy managed to harpoon his first seal on the ice, it marked an important coming-of-age for him as a hunter. As the animal was hauled up through the hole, the boy was told by his father and fellow-hunters to strip himself to the waist. He was then made to lie face-down on the ice – his naked skin seared by the intense cold – while the dying seal was dragged across him, flesh over flesh. That way, it was believed, the seal would come to know his killer, and lose his fear of him for the future.

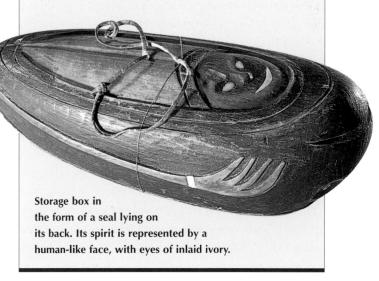

Storage box in the form of a seal lying on its back. Its spirit is represented by a human-like face, with eyes of inlaid ivory.

him loose, to roam the open sea. Yet the little whale never forgot his mother or his human kinsfolk: he regularly guided his whale brethren into inshore waters, within reach of the community's harpoons. Their neighbours, however, envied their good fortune: so much so that one day they hunted down the little whale and killed him out of sheer spite, inaugurating a long history of enmity between the two peoples. But, although the little whale was now dead, women and whales have retained their special bond. To this day it is a female who calls the whale to come and be killed.

The Kingdom of the Fish

The people of the Arctic knew that any disrespect shown towards animal spirits would not be well received and that the consequences for the community could be disastrous. Cautionary tales were therefore of great importance to each new generation of hunters.

All the way round the rugged coastline of Alaska and on down North America's western seaboard, the first warm breezes of the summer are the signal for the salmon-run to start. Having gathered far out in the ocean, the fish group offshore in their teeming hordes. No one knows by what force of instinct this awesome assemblage is subdivided and deployed, nor how each of its silvery schools manages to seek out its ancestral coast.

Each year as the spring gives way to summer the first salmon begin nosing their way into the estuaries, as if trying to sniff out those lakes and pools, many miles inland, where they were born. At first in a trickle of ones and twos, but very soon surging in their hundreds and their thousands, the salmon come rushing upriver, ever more frantic in their desperation to return home. Once they have spawned, many will die, their reproductive work done. But this does not decrease their determination to win through to that destined end. Waterfalls and rapids will bar their way, but the salmon will leap over them undeterred; otters, bears, mink and other predators will ambush them, but they will thrust on, unswerving in their course.

For all the predators of these northwestern rivers, the salmon-run is a time of plenty and easy living. And for the human population, this summer glut has always been the mainstay of the economic year. Caught by the hundred in nets and traps, some of the salmon are enjoyed fresh, in all their juicy tenderness, but most are filleted, to be dried in the summer sun.

Bountiful though it may be as long as it lasts, the salmon-run is over almost as soon as it has started. Just a few days separate the pioneers from the final stragglers. To miss this moment would be catastrophic for the community, so a close eye is always kept out for the first signs that the run is about to start. Maximizing the haul from the brief bonanza means every individual has to play his or her part. Men and women, young and old – even small children are called upon to help in the frantic flurry of fishing, gutting, cleaning and hanging out to dry. Frenetically fast as they must work, all know that the salmon must nonetheless be treated with respect. The fish would not be willing to return if they realized they would not be received with courtesy and care. Even the youngest child knows that protocol has to be observed: for from the very cradle they understand the consequences of doing otherwise.

The Slighted Salmon

One winter in the very earliest age of the world, a young boy asked his mother for something to eat. She gave him a piece of dried salmon, but he turned up his nose in disdain. He was sick of dried salmon, he told her – it was always mouldy. The salmon spirit took great exception to this remark: he had not come all this way and sacrificed his life to be so insulted. For the moment, however, he let it pass in silence. Next summer when the salmon-run came round, however, and the boy baited a snare for seagulls with salmon guts, the spirit decided that the time had come to teach the cocky little brat a much-needed lesson. Seeing a seagull swooping down to take his bait, the lad eagerly rushed down to the riverside to grab his catch, only to overbalance and fall headlong into the river. Deep beneath the surface he sank, to be caught up in the onrush of the swarming salmon and swept along ever further upstream. Fortunately, the salmon were kind to the lost boy, however badly he might have behaved to them the previous year. They saved him from drowning and taught him how to live in their underwater world.

Things were very different down there and he found out just how strange when he sought to sate his hunger on a meal of salmon eggs. The noble fish recoiled in horror at the sight of this: what humankind craved as a delicacy, they despised as excremental filth. The salmon-people then explained to him that their physical forms were but the canoe in which they paddled their way upstream. The elaborate fish-traps they encountered on their journey were the war-houses of humans, they said: he should give them a wide berth if he were wise. And so, throughout the

next winter, the boy swam with the salmon. By the spring he had learned their lore and been initiated into all their rituals: it was time for him to be restored to his human kinsfolk.

The next summer, accordingly, during the salmon-run, his mother was astonished to find amid the catch a fish wearing the copper neck ring of her missing son. She called for the shaman and had him return her son to his human form. Wise in the ways of the fish now, the youth could tell his people the salmon's every preference: exactly how they should catch, cook and store it for the winter months. Never would the boy's lesson be forgotten, by him or by his descendants – for none dared displease the salmon a second time.

A large Yupik mask representing Takiokook, the king of the salmon, who is responsible for leading his fellow fish into the Kuskokwim River in Alaska.

The Sea Mother's Revenge

Like animals and the forces of nature, the spirits who controlled them could either nourish humans or destroy them, according to their mood. One such was the vengeful spirit of the sea, a female figure who revealed a dangerous ambivalence in the idea of motherhood.

Once there was a little orphan girl named Nuliajuk who was treated with resentment by her guardians and mercilessly teased by her peers. She bore her persecution stoically, but inwardly she seethed.

One day when the community was on the move in search of fresh hunting grounds, the people found themselves at a saltwater inlet. Lashing several kayaks together to make rafts, they swarmed aboard with all their possessions and headed for the other shore. On the raft allotted to the children, however, the bullying of Nuliajuk suddenly got out of hand: she was pushed overboard, and fell with a splash into the sea. She tried to save herself but her cruel playmates pushed her away, laughing and jeering as she coughed and spluttered in the icy water. But just as she seemed to be on the verge of going under, she lunged, and caught hold of the edge of the raft with her fingers. Her tormentors merely smiled and took hold of

their knives. Nuliajuk looked up in horror, still hoping for some spark of pity. Then the children severed her fingers and watched calmly as she slipped beneath the surging waves.

Down she sank to the bottom of the sea, where she became an ocean spirit, the Sea Mother – and into the water fell her fingers too, to turn into floating sea mammals. The seals, the walruses and the whales – all their kind were born of her severed flesh, and all would become the obedient servants of her will. For the sheer force of Nuliajuk's anger made her the strongest of the spirits, and a dangerous enemy of humankind. Storms and heavy seas rose up at her beck and call to belabour those who had abused her.

Huge boulders of ice tumble into the surf during a storm at Savissivik, northwest Greenland. Such incidents were blamed on the anger of Nuliajuk, a young orphan persecuted by her peers.

The Whale-Hunt

Even when the Sea Mother gave her progeny to humankind, the harvesting of a whale was still fraught with hardship and danger.

The Sea Mother did not give up her life-forms lightly, even when all due rites had been scrupulously observed. The boat in which the Inuit whaling-party travelled was built not for solidity but for speed, so the fluke of a thrashing tail would smash it, or a snarled harpoon line pull it under in seconds.

Much of the skill in whaling lay in guessing precisely where the whale would surface, for getting it wrong could mean a long and often fruitless pursuit. But even if the whale did rise obligingly beside the boat, success was still not assured. The harpooner had to rely on the steersman to keep his position steady in the swelling sea. The target was also small and fast-moving, for only the heart, or a single point between neck vertebrae, guaranteed a clean kill. Once the harpoon struck home, the hunters had to track the beast on its dying journey. Sealskins, stitched up and inflated, acted as drag-floats for the line of hide, both impeding and indicating the whale's ever-slowing progress.

Mask of a spirit, half-man, half-whale, worn during ceremonies designed to bring success in the whale-hunt.

She governed the comings and goings of land animals too: the caribou and other creatures the Inuit depended on for food and clothing. A word from her, and land and sea animals alike would forsake their normal haunts, leaving the community which had displeased her to starve.

Nuliajuk also controlled misfortunes and misadventures. A fatal fall through unreliable ice, the capsizing of a kayak, death by exposure for the traveller caught out by a sudden storm; disasters such as these could strike the most seasoned Arctic-dweller – but all knew better than to attribute them to accident or chance.

The Sea Mother was also believed to control certain epidemic diseases. Living in small, scattered groups in vast territories, nomadic hunters were generally far less vulnerable to such outbreaks than more settled communities. In the Arctic, however, scattered groups of hunters tended to band together into larger groups to sit out the worst of the winter months, effectively grounded by the elements. The system provided a certain safety in numbers, allowing for communal co-operation and the hunting of the biggest game. But it did open Arctic-dwellers to the risk of infection: epidemics could rage unchecked at such vulnerable times.

The story of Nuliajuk is told by the Netsilik Inuit, who live on and around King William Island off the Arctic coast of Canada. Yet stories such as hers are told throughout the territories of the North American and Asian Inuit – and recognizably related tales can be found among the other peoples of coastal Siberia. The girl goes under many different names, from Takanakapsaluk to Sedna, and her story may vary in significant details (often, for instance, she is killed by a father angry at her refusal to marry as he wishes), but in its essentials, and most of all in its terrible cruelty, it remains substantially the same.

Terror of the Arctic

Of all the animals of the Arctic regions, only one was humankind's rival: the polar bear. Each was to the other both hunter and prey, but on the great ice-sheets that served as a stage for their encounters, only the bravest could face the bear or its spirit.

To a southern visitor to Cape Chidley, at Labrador's most northerly point, the Earth seems to come to its end. Savage storms beat the shoreline of a rocky outcrop bleak even by the standards of the Arctic. For nine or ten months of the year the land above would strike the visitor as a dreary vista of unalleviated black and white. Even in the heat of the summer the earth can manage nothing better than a half-hearted tawny hue. For a stranger it is difficult to decide which aspect of the panorama is the more dismal: the monochrome landscape, the gunmetal sea or the dazzling monotony of the ice.

The Inuit saw such things very differently. Familiar as they were with the subtle half-tones of the Arctic landscape, they found life and colour where the visitor saw only inert drabs and duns, and were keenly sensitive to the ever-changing textures of ice and sea. Yet even those local to the region found Cape Chidley unsettling, shunning it as a place that was both abandoned and cursed. For it was out here, according to the legend, that the terrible Tornarssuk had his home, in a cave deep among the rocks. Most animal spirits were regarded by the Inuit as potential friends, but only the most powerful shamans could form a relationship with Tornarssuk. Greatest of the animal spirits, and far and away the most fearsome, Tornarssuk was the mighty polar bear.

Equally at home charging over rock or ice or swimming strongly through a surging sea, the polar bear is perhaps the least predictable of the Arctic predators. That he is also beyond any doubt the most powerful and aggressive is the Arctic-dweller's misfortune: he is the only predator in the region who hunts human beings for food. Rearing high on his hind legs, the angry polar bear is a truly terrifying sight; in height, weight and sheer ferocity he dwarfs any human unlucky enough to have to face him. The spirit of the polar bear was also strong and severe, an irascible taker of offence and unstinting meter out of punishments. Small wonder then that certain nineteenth-century Danish missionaries in Greenland took Tornarssuk to be an Inuit supreme being – or that others were as quick to identify him with the Devil.

Though not really an all-seeing or all-powerful quasi-Christian divinity or demon, Cape Chidley's presiding spirit did indeed exercise a compelling hold on the life of Labrador's men and women. For he had power over the ghosts of the caribou on which they depended for food for much of the year, and determined whether or not they would have good hunting. When times were hard and game scarce, it was up to the shaman to venture where other mortals feared to tread: in his mystic flight he journeyed to Cape Chidley to visit the spirit in his lair and attempt to propitiate him.

In other Inuit territories many different versions of this same basic myth were to be found, though all agreed upon the polar bear's terrifying power. Like all the best enmities, though, the Inuit's distrust of the polar bear was tinged with respect and even admiration: a beast of such strength and sagacity was worth emulating. It was widely acknowledged that the technique of hunting for seals at their breathing holes in the ice was first learned from the polar bear. The Inuit hunter took the polar bear as his model in more general

Whale vertebra carved into the face of a mighty polar bear, 20th century. Following Inuit tradition, the natural essence of the material has been respected, for the piece can also be seen as two whales arching together – a favourite visual pun of many Inuit carvers.

terms too. Each the other's only natural predator, man and bear found themselves perched side by side at the summit of the Arctic food chain; it was inevitable that the two species should find a certain kinship in competition.

While most animal spirits tended to be regarded as humanity's equals, the sort of soul Inuit folklore attributed to the bear was clearly more powerful than that bestowed on other creatures. As a cultic creature, only the whale, the most valuable of the denizens of the deep, was held in as high regard as the bear – and it has been suggested that the ceremonies of the whale cult originated in rites established earlier for the polar bear.

The Tornarssuk legend was often linked with stories of the Sea Mother – the only spirit to rival him in strength or vengefulness. One variant found in Labrador had it that the polar bear, just like the seals, walruses and whales, was formed from one of her severed fingers. Unable to forgive humanity for the mutilation which brought him into being, he has been at war with them unremittingly ever since. In still other versions of the myth, however, Tornarssuk and the Sea Mother were competitors in malevolence, vying with one another for power over humankind. The coast of Baffin Island, local legend had it, was once swept by a terrible tidal wave after adherents of the two different cults quarrelled over whose spirit was superior. Unable to resist intervening in person, the Sea Mother sent the giant wave crashing towards the shore where it wrought death and destruction. So successful was her show of strength that Tornarssuk retreated to his cave and did not emerge for several years.

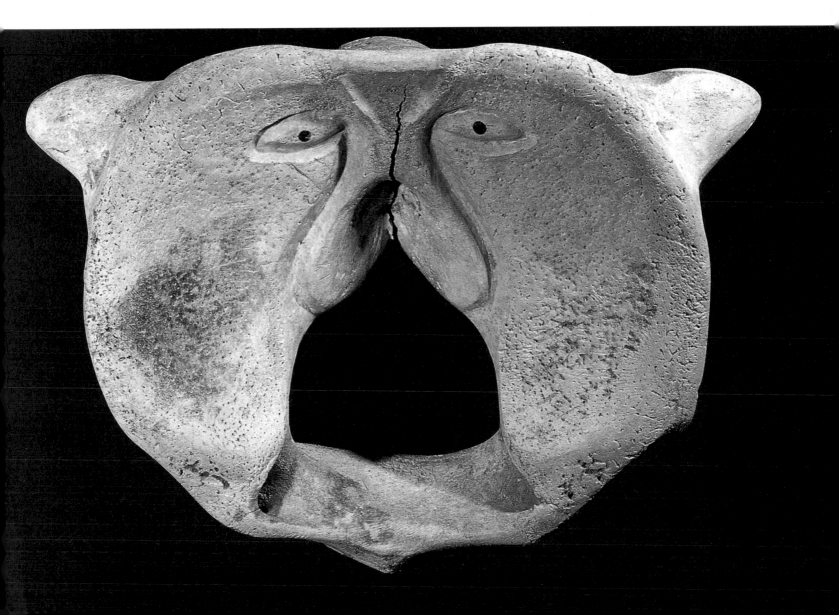

Hunter, Lover, Father, Friend

The relationship between hunter and hunted was imagined by Arctic peoples in many ways. Some saw the two linked as master and servant, others as father and son, or even as lovers. All agreed, however, on the intimacy of the bond between the stalker and his quarry.

The young hunter had never thought to see his quarry as an individual being like himself. Suddenly, though, there she was, a beautiful girl, out walking with her family on the tundra: her two brothers strolling nearby, her loving father and mother bringing up the rear. What had been a knot of grazing caribou was now apparently a group of people like himself. The boy let his bow fall in perplexity and indecision as, ignoring the impatient hisses of his father and brothers, he hung suspended in the existential space between two communities, two wholly different views of the world.

A moment later and he had crossed over entirely – now he no longer remembered that he had ever been a human being. Why should he?

For now, as he looked around him on the tundra, it was human beings, not animals, he saw. They wore clothes like men and women, each one draped in a long white cape, and spoke to one another just the same. They were, in short, indistinguishable from the men and women among whom the boy had spent his life until now – except, that is, for the caribou girl he had fallen in love with. She outdid all others in her grace and beauty. No other woman could conceivably have

Apart from the dog, the caribou, shown here grazing by a winter camp, was the only Arctic animal that could be domesticated by humans. This led to a special bond developing between them.

matched her in face or figure – or in the unfathomable longing of her lustrous brown eyes. His reverie was rudely interrupted, however, as a shout rang out on the crisp, cold air: his beloved's father crying out in urgent alarm. The youth looked up to see strange, fur-clad creatures, reared up high on their hind legs, advancing warily over the tussocky ground towards them, each holding some strange implement in its claw-like forepaws. What they might be he had no idea, but there could be no doubting their sinister intent.

An arrow shaft straightener with incised scenes featuring caribou and three carved heads at the ends, all of which are intended to make the animals more amenable to being caught. Fossil mammoth ivory, Alaska, 19th century.

The group he had joined broke and ran – but too late to get out of range of a foe who raised his weapon to send some swift-flying missile through the air. As his fellows fled, the youth saw one of his loved one's brothers struck and watched as he stumbled momentarily, let his hide fall to earth as if it was just some cape, then ran on with the rest undaunted. As the youth looked back over his shoulder from a safe distance, he saw the strange predators clustered round the garment where it lay on the ground. They seemed to believe they had captured something of great value. Their exuberance ebbed away, though, as they looked about them. They had lost one of their own party.

The caribou, meanwhile, continued calmly on their way home. The youth made the journey with them, his human origins forgotten forever – and in time he would be married to his caribou girl.

This story, told by natives of Labrador, highlights one of the most striking aspects of the Arctic hunters' world-view: their deep identification with the animals they hunted and killed. The caribou might inhabit a separate plane of existence, but socially and culturally they had identities as marked as those of the story-tellers themselves. Practically, such empathy encouraged the hunter to think like his quarry; at the symbolic and ritual levels, however, the identification went much deeper. Among the Mistassini Cree of Canada's James Bay coast, the hunter felt for the caribou he stalked much as he would for a human girl he was wooing. The beaver too was regarded as a lover, but one much more coy in her ways: soft blandishments and much persistence were required to win her. The bear, on the other hand, was regarded in a filial light, either as a beloved son or daughter, or a revered yet aged parent.

Other Algonquin peoples, however, were more likely to see animal societies in terms of dominance and subordination. The analogy here was with man and his domestic dogs. But the place of man in this relationship was taken by a spirit master or mistress, a powerful supernatural being who, like the Inuit Sea-Mother, had complete control over whole species of animals and could give or withhold them on whim. Just as the hunter controlled his dogs, so the spirit master had his "pets" in hand, looking out for their welfare and instructing them in their behaviour.

Another common model for man's relationship with the animals was that of human friendship, an understanding which took time and trust to build. The man who had success in hunting some particular species was thus assumed to have made it his personal friend. His advice and influence were sought after by all the hunters of his community whenever they wished to set out after his "pet". An old man as a rule – it took many years to win an animal's confidence – he was an asset highly treasured by his community. When the time came for him to die, his loss was deeply mourned – not least because it was feared that he would take his friend with him.

Raised by Nature

No inland animal was respected more profoundly by the peoples of the north – particularly those in Siberia – than the brown bear and the most elaborate hunting rituals were used to celebrate its capture. Some regional tales, however, suggested that the bond between humankind and this beast was especially close.

Three Inuit sisters were out gathering berries in the woods one summer's day when the heavens opened and the rain came cascading down. Searching urgently for shelter, they spotted a cave among some rocks. Squeezing in, they sat there panting while the cloudburst continued. Only after they had got their breath back did they begin to look around their sanctuary: all about them lay scattered bones and in the air hung the unmistakable musk of the forest bear. Then they heard the sound of their unwitting host making its way home through the undergrowth outside.

Suddenly, a shaft of light revealed a small hole in the cavern roof, and two of the sisters squeezed their way through to safety. The third, however, was heavily pregnant, and pull and push as she might, she could not get through. Cornered in the cave, she was duly killed and eaten. But the bear, a female, took pity on the little boy whom she found in his mother's womb. She fed and protected the child and brought him up as her own, teaching him all the lore and woodcraft of the bear he assumed he was.

The boy grew up a skilled and enterprising hunter and began roaming ever further afield in search of game. One day his wanderings took him to the coast and there he saw animals he had never seen before – they walked upright and seemed as naked as himself beneath their suits of skins. When he got home he asked his mother what these creatures could have been: they were men, the she-bear told him, and they would kill him without hesitation. She then advised the boy to steer well clear of their encampment. Chilled though he was by his bear-mother's warning, the boy's curiosity could not be restrained and time and again he found himself drawn back to the Inuit village.

It was not long before the men and women spotted him. They talked to their young visitor, asking him

A Yupik dance stick with a figure of a bear. It would have been carried in ritual dances by those who had been successful in hunting and who wished to pay their respects to the spirit of the bear.

who he was and where he came from. As he told them his story they realized that this must be the son of the pregnant woman who had been killed by a bear. Sensing a bond with these people, the boy wanted to join them. Much as he had loved his bear-mother, he found he believed the tale the humans told. Taking the bow his grandfather gave him, he went back to the woods, and there he confronted and killed the bear who had brought him up. He then went back to live with his human kinsfolk, bringing with him great strength, and all the skills and sagacity of the forest bear.

Great Father of the North

The sense that the bear might stand in some quasi-parental relation to its hunters was shared by peoples throughout the circumpolar region. The euphemisms by which the bear was referred to by most of the peoples of the far north – "old man", "big brother", "uncle", "grandad", "short-tail" – acknowledged that it was too dangerous and unpredictable a predator to be named openly.

Yet the people's wariness was tempered with respect and an inescapable feeling of kinship. Hence, perhaps, the excuses so frequently offered to the bear when it was killed. It was not we who killed you, the Tungus of central Siberia were at pains to assure their quarry; it must have been Russians, acting through us by devilish European enchantment.

Yet like many other Siberian peoples, the Tungus were enthusiastic aficionados of the bear-hunt and constructed lavish festivities around its successful completion. The very form of the hunt lent itself to elaborate ceremonial in a way in which other sorts of hunting tended not to. Typically, the hunt fell into two distinct stages which could be enacted several months apart. The bear would first be tracked down to its den deep in the forest. A second expedition would later make straight for this hiding place and provoke the bear into emerging to face a row of spears or rain of arrows.

Often the hunt took advantage of the rhythms of the bear's own year, the quarry being trailed to its lair through the first fresh snows on the eve of its hibernation, then tackled as it emerged, weak and sleepy, the following spring.

Breastfeeding the Bear Cub

Ensuring a bear was dispatched into the next world with favourable reports of its earthly hosts was a prime concern for many Arctic peoples, especially in some parts of Siberia.

Many eastern Siberian peoples kept captured cubs in cages to be paraded and then killed at later bear festivals. Until then they were regarded as honoured guests, to be pampered in every way by the community's women. But of all Siberia's bear lovers, none went quite so far as the Orochon, whose women actually breastfed the smaller bear cubs.

The community's families took turns feeding and watering the bear and taking it for walks in the forest. The reasons for such indulgence were clear – and were spelled out to the animal as it faced death: after such treatment, the bear was obliged to carry a favourable report of its hosts into the next world. The community had done all it could, now it was time for the bear to give something in return. Game and fish in plenty for the winter, freedom from sickness and death, and good fortune for all – such were the benefits bestowed by a satisfied bear.

The bear-hunt's denouement was a well-rehearsed ritual, enacted in a familiar location, not improvised on the run as occurred in most other forms of hunting.

The Range of Bear Rites

As outside observers described the events earlier this century, the death of the bear was the signal for a long and varied set of rites to begin. When Khant, also known as the Ostyak, hunters of western Siberia's Ob River region killed a bear, for example, they first flung snow – or in summer, moss or earth – at one another. They then laid out their victim on its back, placing sticks vertically on its belly to suggest the opening of a suit. This "clothing" was then removed, but the skin of the head and forepaws was left intact out of respect.

The bearskin and body were then borne separately back to the hunters' camp, where women were busy preparing for the bear's reception. A bed of bark was made up at the hunter's house and the carcass stretched out, its chin resting comfortably between its forepaws.

Images of deer, in bread or birchbark, were then placed before it, and rings placed upon its claws if it was a female. Silver coins were used to cover the animal's eyes, and a muzzle of birchbark to close its mouth, lest the community's women should look it in the eye or kiss it on the lips – both male prerogatives. In fact, the women had to cover their faces with handkerchiefs as the bear was carried into camp: it was taboo to face it directly, and they had much to do getting ready for the festivities.

The Hunter's Celebrations

The revelry hosted by the hunter was supposed to last five nights or even longer for an adult male bear, four for a female, and three nights for a bear cub. Men were often bankrupted by such celebrations, but none would dream of opting out: no higher honour could be won by a tribesman of the Khant people.

Flushed with pride – and increasingly with drink – the lucky hunter sat himself to the right of his trophy, his left hand resting proprietorially on the animal's neck. Opposite him, to the left of the bear, musicians played festive music as guests began to trickle in from far afield. Each new arrival greeted the bear with a kiss on the snout, although the women had to be sure to do so only through a handkerchief. Song, dance and drinking were thenceforth the order of the night; bawdiness and irreverence the rule. While some songs and dance steps clearly commemorated the bear, gave thanks for its killing and expressed hope for future bounty, many simply satirized Russian officialdom or mocked members of the community. Often men dressed up as women, turning the normal social order upside-down.

At some stage during the proceedings the bear-slayer walked out into the darkness with his bow, then turned to face his house and shot an arrow at it; the higher up it hit the timbers, the sooner he would kill his next bear. A more direct way of divining the future was to ask the dead bear itself, its killer whispering the names of the men present in its ear then tweaking the heavy hide and trying to raise it. The man at whose name the hide lifted easily was destined for success, for the outcome of all bear hunts to come had already been preordained.

The festivities over for the night, the bear was borne outside to preside over daytime sports: wild snowball-fights and wrestling matches. The women remained indoors, although they too did battle with water and snow. While much of the bear's flesh was eaten in the course of the festivities, certain important parts were kept to be eaten by the two sexes separately under the strictest ritual conditions. The men adjourned to the woods to eat the head, the heart and the paws, while the women ate the hindquarters in the hunter's home. The meal over, the hands and mouth had to be wiped with wood shavings which were then carefully burned along with any leftover meat: no part of the bear could suffer the indignity of being scavenged by dogs.

The Boy Taken by Wolves

Many of the tales about the close relationship between animals and humans concerned other forms of wildlife which offered as much potential danger as the bear, and there was always the possibility that the relationship would go wrong and lead to disaster.

An Inuit couple had a baby boy, the joy of his father and mother. But so fine a boy was he that he was coveted by wolves: they determined not to be denied him. One afternoon, therefore, a he-wolf slipped out of his skin and approached the boy's parents, appearing to them in the form of a naked man. As his wife looked on, the wolf-man suggested that they too should strip off their clothes. He sang a strange song, and before they knew it they were undressed and dancing. They were jerked back to startled consciousness, however, when the wolf abruptly ceased his spell; his wolf-wife had the child and it was time for him to run off and join her.

Seeing the big grey wolf loping away, the horrified couple turned as one to look for their son: they saw his empty cradle, and at once knew what had happened. Resolving to track their child's abductors down, they armed themselves, each with a bow. They would need to bring down both male and female wolf in a single instant if they were to ensure the boy's safety. All day they searched without result, until suddenly, quite by chance, they stumbled upon a rocky ravine in which the wolves were playing with their little "boy cub". Waiting till the strange family slept, the man and woman raised their bows and let loose their arrows: both wolves were killed – but so too was their sleeping infant. So tightly had the she-wolf been holding him in her love that a single shaft had pierced both bodies right through. Dutifully, the boy's parents bore their dead child off home for burial.

The Wisdom of the Wilderness

Whether from the prudent wisdom of the beaver, the quick-witted resourcefulness of the squirrel or the laughable folly of the hare, humankind could learn much from the animals and from their constant battles with their neighbours and their environment.

The great Dene shaman Yamoria once spent a year as a beaver, living in a lake in his native northwestern Canada. He marvelled to see the industry and patience with which his fellow beavers strove all summer long just to prepare for the hardships of the winter. One whole day they spent collecting mud and stones to reinforce their lodge, making it so thick and strong that it became impregnable. When, driven to desperation by winter hunger, some wolverine or bear decided to claw his way into the beavers' refuge, the sheer scale of the task would now defeat him. And day after summer day, when it seemed the whole forest was a feast of food, the beavers refused to relax and take things easy. Instead they stacked up logs by the hundred outside their home, a store against the scarcities of winter.

As if to make things still harder for themselves, moreover, the beavers ignored those trees which were closest at hand, choosing instead to venture far into the forest to bring home timber. When Yamoria asked them why they went to all this trouble when there were so many trees nearby, they told him they were saving those for when the heavy snows made travel impossible. And so indeed, when the Arctic winter began to make life so harsh for so many creatures, the beavers were living a life of ease and abundance. How much men might learn from them, mused Yamoria.

Another tale, however, signals the disaster attendant upon a singular lack of prudence. It concerns Siksik, a squirrel for whom summer was one joyous spree which she spent eating and eating, until she grew round and fat. One afternoon, as she was working her way through an extensive berry patch, Okpik the owl swooped down and

A Yupik owl mask with an *inua* face peering from its back. In one tale this wise animal was outwitted by a squirrel.

only very narrowly missed her. Siksik went lolloping off towards the safety of her home but, fat and breathless as she was, she made painfully slow progress. Toiling up the treetrunk to her door, she found to her consternation that she was unable to squeeze inside. As Okpik came gliding in again, Siksik was forced to run back down the tree and conceal herself at ground-level in some nearby undergrowth. Smiling, Okpik settled down to wait out her portly prey: sooner or later Siksik would have to come home, and when she did, the owl decided, she would be waiting.

But if Siksik lacked far-sightedness, she was by no means short of resourcefulness or presence of mind; even now her initial panic was rapidly abating. Reckoning that her persecutor, who was nocturnal by nature, would wilt in the hot summer sun, she decided to wait where she was until Okpik had become quite drowsy. When the squirrel finally made her move and darted as quickly as she could for safety, the owl did indeed take several seconds to shake off her sluggishness. Okpik was still too quick for a fat squirrel, though, and just as Siksik was squeezing herself through her door, the owl got a claw to her rump and tore off the squirrel's bushy tail.

Siksik felt naked without it and determined to get it back. Asking her children to plead with Okpik for its return, she suggested that they offer the owl something to eat as an inducement – instead of the expected meaty morsel, though, she substituted a hard stone. They did as their mother asked, throwing Okpik their offering for the tail's return. The owl caught the pebble with a snap – and promptly broke her beak. So badly was she hurt that soon afterwards she died, and Siksik, reunited with her beloved tail, wandered through the forest swishing it this way and that, grateful for the cunning that had outwitted the great, wise owl.

Neither sensible nor clever but vainglorious and absurd, the hare is nevertheless an instructive example, as one Siberian story recounted. In the first age of the world,

Antlers bring a protective charm to this bentwood tub which would have been used for hauling water or holding food. For the hare, however, they brought nothing but trouble.

apparently, the hare's ears were not the long, elegant lugs they are today but short, stubby protuberances. The only difference between his ears and the other animals was that his were exercised far more than theirs. An inquisitive creature who minded everybody's business but his own, he found himself one day eavesdropping on a conversation between a great elk and his wife in a forest clearing. The time had come to cast off his antlers, the deer confided, but he was loath to simply throw them away and he was wondering whether they might be useful to another animal.

The hare could not restrain himself; leaping up out of the grass, he begged that he, the hare, be allowed the old antlers. Surprised as the deer was at this strange request, he saw no reason to refuse it. He gave the hare the antlers and stared with astonishment as he put them on. The silly creature strutted and swaggered up and down the clearing, ridiculously pleased with himself. The hare now thought himself king of the woods, even though his new antlers were several times bigger than he himself was. All of a sudden, a pine cone fell down on his head and gave him such a fright that he leaped up in alarm and bolted headlong for the nearest thicket. There his antlers became hopelessly entangled with bushes and brambles: he could move neither forwards nor backwards. Roaring with laughter at this absurd spectacle, the elk removed the hare's antlers which would be no use, he said, to someone who was as scared as he was – he would never hang around long enough to lock antlers with anyone. The elk then replaced them with great long ears which, he argued, would be much more appropriate for an animal who was so inquisitive and so interested in eavesdropping.

A Land of Gifts

While the souls of animals may, if adequately appeased, offer themselves up to the respectful hunter, bonds between man and beast can be forged deeper still – for in many stories of the Arctic peoples, animals repay human kindness with unexpected boons.

A certain Siberian hunter would sometimes take his young son with him on his long forays into the forest. On one trip, however, a tiger appeared to the hunter in a dream and declared his intention to eat the young boy. He instructed the hunter to leave the child in the woods as an offering, or prepare to be eaten himself. The man woke up in a cold sweat: he could hardly dream of saving his own life at the expense of his beloved son's, but if he disobeyed the beast, his wife and his other children would be left without their provider – and even then there was no guarantee that his son would be saved. So, sick to his soul, he resigned himself to his loss and set off wearily through the forest, leaving the sleeping child behind.

It was mid-morning by the time the boy awoke. Rubbing his eyes and blinking he looked round for his father – and found himself transfixed by the smouldering eyes of a ferocious tiger. At once he leaped up into a nearby tree and started climbing, scrambling frantically upwards with the great cat crashing through the branches behind him. The branches began to thin, and soon the boy found himself at the top. He looked fearfully down – but saw that the tiger had become ensnared between two branches below. The boy made his way back down to the ground and safety, skirting warily past the furious beast. He then sat down by the spent campfire to wait for his father's return.

All that day he stayed there, but his father did not come back. At last he began to tire, and since the trapped tiger had given up its roaring and now simply whined pathetically in the tree, the boy lost his fear and felt it safe to settle down to sleep. That night, however, the tiger appeared to him in a dream, pleading with him to spare his life and promising rich rewards in return. When the boy awoke the following morning, he took his axe and felled the tree in which the tiger was caught. Once more at ground-level, the great cat was able to wriggle free. Seeing the fearsome beast again at such close quarters, the boy began to have misgivings about what he had done, but his fears were needless for the tiger simply shambled off into the forest. That night he appeared again in the boy's dreams. He thanked him sincerely for his help, and suggested that the next morning he set traps for sable. Before laying each one, he should describe a ring around it with his sleeve to ensure good hunting. And so it turned out: sleek sable seemed to be fighting to enter his traps. As the rich pelts stacked up ever higher beside the boy's tent, he rejoiced in his good fortune and was thankful that he had decided to trust the tiger. But he was still worried about his father's continued absence.

The unhappy man had been trying for weeks to get up his nerve to come back and gather his son's remains for burial. When he did set off for the clearing, however, he was astonished to find his son sitting there as large as life amid a veritable mountain of sable. As he hugged the boy he marvelled at the incredible generosity of the tiger – a blessing which would assure his family's prosperity forever. But the tiger's most precious gift was not of course a stack of skins but his honoured promise to spare the life of a beloved son.

While this Siberian folktale was intended to entertain, it also embodies an important aspect of the Arctic world-view. The gratitude of the animal reflects the give and take that underlies the whole natural, and economic, order. The boy's shift in attitude towards the tiger, from fear to trust, articulates the bond between man and nature: "the Old Agreement", ancient and inviolable.

The Relation Who Was a Wolf

Feared hunter of the tundra and kinsman to the domestic dog, the wolf's image among the Inuit was nothing if not ambivalent. Many tribes tell the story of the man out hunting in the first age of the world, who was helped by a wolf who turned out to be his brother-in-law.

Times were hard and the man found he was setting his snares in vain – but traps were all the weapons he had at his disposal in those days before the bow and arrow. Day after day he had trudged through the deep snow to check them, his progress painful and slow – since nobody had yet invented snowshoes. The thought of his hungry wife and children, cold and miserable at home, drove him on – but despair was slowly sapping his will to continue.

Suddenly he came to a blazing fire, in whose cheery light he saw a stranger, tending a bubbling pot of some savoury supper. He was Wolf, the man said, and he was actually the hunter's brother-in-law. This campfire and food were for him, his valued relative; here were several caribou Wolf had killed to feed and clothe his sister's family. Here too were some snowshoes which would make his homeward trek so much easier. Greatest gift of all,

however, was the bow and arrow he gave the man – now he could supplement the rabbits he trapped with bigger game such as elk and caribou.

Joyfully the man thanked Wolf for his wonderful generosity and they laughed and joked together far into the night. At last, however, the hunter fell asleep exhausted. He awoke just in time to see a dark form slinking off into the morning mist: his benefactor and brother-in-law, a real wolf!

THE MAGIC OF THE SEAMSTRESS

Just as the male preserve of hunting fused practicality and symbolism, so the woman's art of sewing was imbued with ritual significance. Each community had its own designs that might reflect myths or legends. So a patch of brown fur on a hood of white rabbit pelt might represent a bear seated on a mountain; or red beads on a tassel might respect the memory of the wounded Yupik hero Apanuugpak. In a culture which created harmony from the rival elements of matter and spirit, human and animal, clothing served a purpose beyond the practical: for through the use of designs, symbols and materials, the Arctic peoples became bound to one another, to their environment and to the spirit of the dead animals themselves.

Left: Beaded Inuit woman's cap. Beads were a sign of wealth and prestige; the Inuit called them *sapangaq* or "precious stones". Acquired by trade from the 17th century onwards, the beads were threaded on sinew and were often used to decorate headdresses.

Above: Designs for clothes or fabrics might be determined by the status of the owner, the hide the material was cut from or the purpose for which the piece was made. The pattern on this storage bag, made from seagull's feet and bleached sealskin, symbolizes the sun, or light. The receptacle was used to hold moss with which to make the wicks for seal-oil lamps.

Below: Beads were also used to embroider clothes, like this Inuit woman's *amautik,* or parka. Such intricate work helped display the skill of the seamstress.

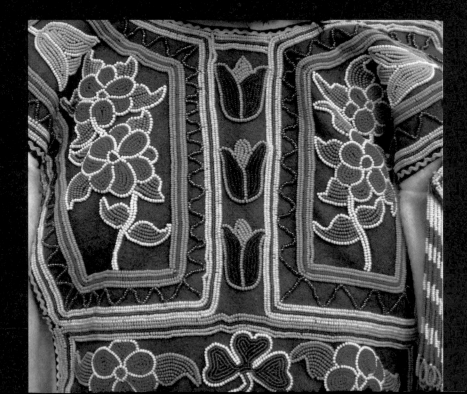

Left: Inuit women photographed in traditional costume on board a ship at Cape Fullerton in the Northwest Territories, *c.*1903–1904. These women would have learned how to make their first *amautik* from their mothers and grandmothers. Such was the significance accorded these articles of clothing that if even a small mistake was spotted, the whole piece would be taken apart and remade.

Above: A seal-gut parka. Such coats were the embodiment of magic and utility: testament to the seamstress's skill, they were perfectly waterproof, and also lent the wearer the physical skin of the seal the hunters stalked. Among the Aleut the sea mammal spirits were honoured by wearing highly decorated gutskin *kamleika*. Many North American groups traded gut parkas (seal, sea lion or walrus) to the Chukchi in Siberia who wore them during ceremonies to honour Keretkun, the walrus god and Master of the Sea.

Right: Aivilingmiut Iglulik woman's inner parka, or *amautik*, early 20th century. Such garments were made by a woman after the birth of her first child. The design was highly symbolic, particularly referring to the female as a giver of life. The apron represents childbirth; the wrist and shoulder designs symbolize tattoos. The triangles and lines are traditional Thule-culture patterns whose exact meaning has been lost.

TRICKSTERS, CULTURE HEROES AND SHAMANS

The people of Tikigaq, in northwestern Alaska, say that many years ago their divine ancestor, Tulunigraq, was fashioned from lamp oil by an old woman. But when she gave him human form she also provided him with a raven's beak. Almost at once he embarked on a series of adventures in which he was by turns mischievous trickster, creator and culture hero – a teacher of survival skills to his people. He was also a shaman, the religious specialist called upon by Arctic peoples to end famine or fight illness by conjuring spirits.

Many heroes who accomplish such feats, however, use their supernatural powers to serve their own ends – and the stories of Arctic mythology celebrate the trickster both as powerful creator and lazy soul who wants little more than a free meal, copious sex and a long sleep.

Arctic tradition is rich in tales of shamans. They embark on journeys to spirit realms when the community needs their special help. Sometimes they travel as part of their initiation as shamans, and return to the world of humans full of arcane knowledge. At others, they journey in order to visit powerful spirits who have the capacity to restore the balance in the natural world that has been knocked askew by human wrongdoing.

In many tales, the shaman can be found using his powers indiscriminately, like a trickster. Aquppak, a man from Tikigaq who became a powerful shaman after being kidnapped by whale spirits for one whole winter (see page 77), later tried to pull a mean-spirited trick on his fellow hunters. When the meat from a whale was being shared out, it was traditional for all involved to take an equal share, no matter what part they had played in the kill. Aquppak would make sure that his share had been brought onto the land from the iceberg where it was being cut up, then use his power to make the ice drift out to sea so his companions lost their portion. But the next time the hunters outwitted the shaman: they made him believe that his share was still on the ice – making sure that he did not make the iceberg drift out. The trickster was outdone in trickery.

Opposite: The cover of a Nanai shaman's drum, made from birchbark, cotton and leather. Beating such an instrument would help summon the spirits depicted on its face.

Below: The sun rises over the vast and forbidding icescape. In such remote places it is easy to appreciate how the peoples of the Arctic sensed spirits stalking their lands.

The Changing Faces of the Soul

Silence and solitude brought Arctic peoples into a close and intense relationship with the land, which they considered to be full of spiritual power. Spirit, they said, moved through all things and had many different aspects – it was in the land and its animals, the sea and its manifold creatures, as well as in humans themselves.

Although hunters came together to share out the spoils, they usually hunted alone. Some believed that enduring solitude, hardship and danger brought access to the truth of a hidden reality. In lonely places far from any settlement, shamans had fierce encounters with helper spirits that marked a stage in their initiation (see box, opposite).

The people viewed animals as creatures worthy of deep respect. But the division between humans and animals could be crossed, for both people and creatures had souls. Each animal's soul

Like all animals, caribou possessed a human-like soul that could reveal itself at any time. Such a belief is reflected in this wooden figure of a caribou with a human head made by the Bristol Bay Inuit, Bering Sea, *c*.1882.

was called its *inua*. In Alaska, the Yupik people made remarkable shamanic masks of fish, birds and sea creatures showing the *inua* as a human face. *Inua* literally means "his (or her) man", the person within each beast.

In the world of myth creatures could switch from animal to human and back again. In day-to-day reality, people and animals appeared to have fixed, separate forms but the potential for change was understood. Throughout the cycles of Raven, Crow and Beaver-man the heroes can assume or cast off human form at will. Many tales recount ordinary people's encounters with animals in human form. Sometimes, however, these encounters had disastrous consequences.

The Polar Inuit told of a woman who left her husband when she had had enough of his beatings. She walked far from the village and came across a strange house. When she entered it she found a mother polar bear in human form, who welcomed her. The woman lived with the bear and her offspring for some time, but eventually returned to her own village. Before she left she promised the bear-woman she would not reveal where the house was, but as soon as she reached home she told her husband what she had found. He set off with his fellow hunters to kill the beasts.

Watching him go, the woman felt afraid and hid beneath the sleeping platform – but through her special powers the bear knew what she had done and plotted revenge. When the hunters called she was not at home, for she was paying a grim visit to the woman who had betrayed her. The disappointed hunter returned to his village to find his wife's body horribly mangled and thrown on the rubbish heap.

At One With the Animals

When a human took the shape of an animal it sometimes marked a stage in their initiation as a shaman. In a tale from northwest Alaska, the soul of a Tikigaq man named Aquppak lived among the whales for a whole winter and the experience brought him great powers.

An autumn day saw Aquppak walking the deserted strand. It was the time of the whaling ceremonies when wooden carvings of people, whales and other creatures were paraded and burnt to ensure a successful hunt. Suddenly Aquppak encountered a group of strangers about to launch a boat. The men invited him to join them but when he declined they stole his soul. In truth they were not humans but some of the carvings which had come to life.

They carried Aquppak's soul far away out to sea, to the land of the whales. There his soul took the form of a whale and lived among the creatures for the eight long months of winter. He learned that the whales keep a close watch on what people are doing on the Alaskan coast; they wait until they think the hunters are ready and then swim north to meet them. Back on land, in Tikigaq, Aquppak's soulless body lay comatose.

The following spring Aquppak's soul swam north with the whales to the region of Tikigaq. When he saw his relatives out in a boat he offered himself to their harpoon. They rejoiced at the catch although they did not know the whale contained Aquppak's soul. When they brought the whale back to land and cut up its flesh, his soul was released and entered his body again.

Aquppak recovered and found that he now had shamanic powers. When he heard that the Utqiagvik people had murdered his sister Nanautchiaq, he vowed to avenge her.

He changed himself into a snowy owl to bring trouble to the Utqiagvik. The following winter the Utqiagvik saw a great owl haunting their settlement like an angry spirit. Their hunt was unsuccessful and their food supplies spoiled; that winter many Utqiagvik men and women, killers of Nanautchiaq, starved.

The Mischievous Trickster

From Siberia to the Pacific northwest of North America the sharpwitted trickster is a popular mythological figure. He goes by many names, Coyote or Rabbit further south, commonly Raven or Crow in northern regions, but his wily character is always the same.

A trickster is as chaotic as life itself. Sometimes he is a creator, at others a cheat – he will teach survival skills but also loves to cause disruption and conflict for its own sake. His insatiable appetite for food and sex results in unacceptable anti-social behaviour, while at the same time he garners a sneaking admiration for his sheer wantonness.

For many Inuit and northern Pacific peoples Raven was revered as creator of the world and of humankind, and as controller of the wild animals. Hunters laid out offerings of meat for him to ensure propitious weather or good fortune and success in the hunt. Raven amulets were believed to bring the wearer hunting prowess and toughness. In west Greenland, people believed that the loud-voiced raven used its hoarse croaking call to warn reindeer of a hunter's approach, and hunters made offerings of reindeer meat to propitiate the Raven spirit in the hope that they would be permitted to approach their prey unannounced.

According to a tale from eastern Greenland, at one time ravens not people had the power of speech. Such was their mischievous, deceptive nature that the dark birds always spoke in a contrary way, expressing the opposite of their true meaning. If a raven wanted to thank someone, for example, it would open its sharp beak to let loose a stream of abuse. But one day a shaman worked his magic on a raven and wrested from it knowledge of words and how to use them. Ever afterwards people could speak and ravens could only caw. The birds kept their contrary nature and to this day remain quick to anger and prone to noisy mischief.

A myth of the coastal Chukchi revealed how in the days before history Big Raven created land and sea, then filled them with teeming life. It happened that Big Raven's wife, a fine, glossy bird like himself, nagged at him to create the world. But he was not industrious and he would not do it until the day when she transformed herself into a human

A Yupik raven mask from the Yukon, with the head and feet of a real raven mounted on a painted wooden face. Raven was much revered by the peoples of the Arctic, but he was seldom trusted.

Coghill Lake in Alaska. Raven stories are told throughout this region, where the mountain ranges were said to have been created from pieces of his dung.

woman and gave birth to three strong sons. When the boys laughed at Big Raven, he flew away, determined to demonstrate his own creative powers.

He came to the horizon, where air meets land, and there found a great tent pitched on a barren patch of dusty earth. Inside he saw a gathering of men. When one came out, Big Raven asked who had created them. The man said that where sky and earth rubbed together dust had formed and from that dust they had emerged. Big Raven declared that he was on his way to create the great lands of the north and the expansive seas that flowed against them. The man came with him.

The two travelled on until the man pointed out a good place. Then Big Raven dropped some bird dung. As it landed it was transformed into land and became a great continent. Other droppings turned into islands. Big Raven thought his work was done but the man said they still needed mountains and fresh water. Big Raven relieved himself to make lakes and rivers and then excreted to create mountain ranges.

They came to a place where trees grew and Big Raven chopped at them with his hatchet. Chips of wood flew off in all directions: pieces from oak trees became seals, pine chips became walruses and black birch wood took the form of whales. Other chips settled on land and polar bears, reindeer and foxes were soon moving about.

Far and wide the men spread out, but they had no womenfolk until the Spider Woman gave birth to some delicately beautiful human daughters. The man who had flown with Big Raven on his mission of creation took one of these fine-featured maidens to be his wife. But when Big Raven visited them some time later he found that they were sleeping apart. Big Raven called the man outside the tent and went in himself to the woman, who was slumbering naked, her rare beauty uncovered. There the lecherous trickster satisfied himself with her, while the man stood shivering in the cold outside. Finally Big Raven called the man

79

Why Raven is Black

The story of how the raven came to be black all over is told in many variant forms throughout the Arctic region. This version is from southeast Greenland.

The mischievous raven came to be coloured black when the rude trickster fell foul of a diver.

At one time, so the elders say, all the birds were white and they could talk just as people do today. Then the raven and the great northern diver alighted on the towering rocks of the Greenland coast and began to talk about their colouring. The diver complained that its brilliant white plumage made it hard for a bird to approach its prey without being spotted. The raven suggested that they could solve that problem by painting each others' feathers, and the diver immediately agreed.

The raven went first. While the diver sat perfectly still, with its eyes closed, the raven skilfully stained its companion's plumage black, leaving only a few delicate speckles of the original colour. It flew away a few wingbeats to view the pattern from a distance and thought it good work. It told the diver to look – and the bird was very pleased with its new coat. Then the raven stood completely still while the diver eagerly set to work.

The diver was so pleased with the pattern on its own feathers that it copied it exactly in decorating the raven. But when the raven saw the result it spoke roughly, dismissing it as ugly and unattractive. For a moment the diver lost its temper and covered the raven from head to foot in deep glossy black. Then the raven flew away, cawing in rough-voiced anger. It never afterwards consorted with the diver and to the present day the raven has kept its glossy black colouring.

and showed him how to have sexual intercourse. Man and woman set to with gusto, and Big Raven flew away. The next time he visited, a happy child was shouting and playing on the ground outside the house.

A tale told by Yupik groups in Alaska recounts how the insubordinate Raven assumed power over the hunt by inadvertently delivering a whale to some hunters. Having flown into the whale by accident, the Raven listened to the pleas of the whale's *inua* requesting him to move carefully and not endanger the whale's life. Raven, however, couldn't resist doing what he had specifically been asked not to and the great mammal died. When it did so, the creature's huge belly collapsed around Raven. He lay there as the carcass floated on the icy waves, tormented by hunger, listening to the distant cries of the sea birds and remembering with longing the freedom of the skies. Tides brought the whale ashore and a group of Inuit found it. When they sliced the whale open out flew Raven, who then settled upon a rock nearby. Of course he took his share in the division of the spoils. The story explains Raven's power over the hunt and shows why hunters liked to use raven amulets.

The Price of Pride

The Raven was not always seen as all-powerful and there are plenty of tales which show how he got his come-uppance. The Mackenzie Inuit tell how the raven and the loon were disturbed by a passing hunter as they were decorating each other. The loon became very frightened and spilled dark paint all over the raven, leaving him completely black. Some say the loon was going to paint colourful patterns and apply some decorative

In the western Arctic, very few representations were made of untrustworthy Raven. The only evidence of his presence is often a footprint which appears on the bottom of serving bowls such as this one from Norton Sound, Alaska.

detail on top of this dark coat – but it never happened. In an Iglulik version of the same tale, the raven, furious at being covered with black dye, threw a stone at the loon, breaking its legs. This story explains why loons appear to walk with difficulty. All of these tales, however, belong to the rich vein of stories which account for why the raven is black (see box, opposite).

Another widespread myth explains how Raven met his end. It happened that he courted a fine-looking goose, begging her to become his wife. But the goose was unwilling, for she told Raven that he would never survive the long flight across the sea when the time came for the geese to migrate. But at this Raven only laughed and persisted with his courtship. In time the goose gave way and became his wife. In the days before her fellow birds took off on their long journey she tried to persuade Raven to rest, for, she said, he would need all his strength to survive the flight. Raven claimed that his strong wings would never grow tired. Even when the geese themselves rested in preparation for the flight, Raven flew hither and thither in the teeth of the icy wind, with no other reason than to show off.

So when it came to the flight of migration itself, Raven grew desperately tired when they were only halfway to their destination. Soon he could fly no more and sank down to the heaving waves. Raven's wife called to a friend to help her and for as long as they could they supported Raven with their wings. The great black bird was heavy, however, and he eventually sank, cawing pitifully, to his death. In some versions a shaman on a soul journey encountered Raven's spirit and learned the tale of how the great bird was undone by pride and boastfulness.

81

Crow's Dark Designs

In some Arctic regions Raven's many achievements and colourful character are attributed to Crow. Like Raven, Crow is governed by an insatiable appetite for food, is dedicated to idleness and sexual licence – but is also the provider of good things, who teaches humans how to fish and make traps for animals.

For the Tanaina Indians of Alaska and British Columbia, the embodiment of the trickster is not the raven but its close relation, the crow. They tell a lengthy cycle of the bird's adventures which focus repeatedly on its uncontrollable desire to steal and to feast without working for the food.

One sparkling morning, they say, Crow was riding the crisp air high above the Alaskan coastline when on the shore below he saw a giant putting the finishing touches to a sleek, elegant canoe. For a few moments he circled in the air, admiring the giant's handiwork, his mind whirring as he formulated a cunning plan. Then he flew off to alight in a forest some way away. As his feet touched the ground, Crow turned himself into a good-looking young man, his dark feathers transformed into a sweep of glossy black hair. Then he made his way back to where the giant was working. He approached him and began to make conversation during which he repeatedly expressed his admiration for the fine vessel.

The giant was flattered, and when the young man asked for a ride in the boat, he happily agreed. Crow took the canoe out a little way, then came back full of praise for its perfect handling and great speed. Then he bade the giant good evening and went on his way. The following day he returned and took the boat out a little further before bringing it back. On the third day, he rowed right around the point and far up the coast. The giant waited patiently on the beach for the return of his handiwork, but far away Crow cackled with happy laughter, alight with pleasure at having got something for nothing.

As he paddled here and there in the canoe, he sang a lilting song asking other animals if they wanted a ride. Several came forward but he turned all away until he was approached by a fat seal. Now Crow saw where his next meal was coming from: he made friends with the seal and after giving him a ride in the canoe, tempted him ashore with the promise of food. On land he turned himself back into a bird and led the seal deep into the forest.

This hunting hat, from the Bering Sea region, depicts a bird which may be a crow, the sly bird which, with the raven, was seen by many Inuit peoples as the great trickster of Arctic mythology. Wearing such a hat would invoke the bird's cunning. Representations of Crow, however, were rare because of his capricious nature.

There they made camp. Because they could find no food Crow offered to cut off his own foot and exchange it for one of the seal's flippers. The creature agreed and after cutting off the flipper Crow used the wondrous juices of his mouth to heal the wound over. Then they roasted their food over the fire. But whereas the flipper made a juicy meal for the bird, Crow's foot proved a nasty mouthful for his companion and did not satisfy him, only making him desperate with thirst. Crow persuaded the seal to stay in the camp and promised to fetch him water, but he dawdled on his way and when he returned with water deliberately spilled it on the ground right in front of the parched animal.

Now the seal went with Crow to search for more water. When they came to a place where there were three wells, Crow would not let his pretended friend drink from the two nearest, saying that only the third, reserved for renowned hunters and chiefs, was fit for a great figure such as he was. Finally the thirsty creature sank his head into the well and drank deeply. While he did so, Crow leaped on him and began to peck at his back. The seal pulled his head slowly out, heavy with water, but Crow reassured him that he was only cleaning dirt off his skin. Then the seal set to drinking again and Crow pecked a great hole through which he drew out the creature's inner organs. The seal died and Crow settled down to a feast.

Afterwards Crow took human form once more and set off in his stolen canoe. He came upon a village and was immediately tempted by the chance to make some mischief again. Beaching the boat, he wandered close to the village, crying loudly as if stricken with grief. When the curious villagers approached, he told them that his hunting companion, Seal, had choked right in front of him in their forest camp. Crow whipped up a storm of tears which ran down his handsome face. The sympathetic villagers were greatly affected by the grieving stranger and led him to their chief, in whose presence Crow repeated the tale. But just as he was finishing he belched loudly and regurgitated a great chunk of seal blubber. Then the

Implements such as these were used by hunters to scratch the ice to lure seals to the surface of the sea. The wooden scratcher is in the form of a limb with bird's claws attached, while the ivory one represents a seal and has seal claws on its base.

villagers understood what had really happened and turned on him. Crow quickly turned back into a bird and fled, never to be seen again.

Learning from Ingratitude

In a version of a tale also told about Raven (see page 81), Crow was attracted by a fine-looking goose and used all his wiles to persuade her to marry him. When winter approached he tried, like Raven, to fly south with the geese but could not keep up and fell into the icy sea; according to the Tanaina, however, Crow survived the fall by hitching a ride with a great beluga whale. Still he felt nothing for the creature that had saved his life – and even made the beluga the victim of one of his tricks. The whale swam with its eyes beneath the water; perched on the whale's breathing hole Crow shouted down what he could see. As they came close to the shore he told the beluga that the beach was far away and it swam fast and hard. The next instant the whale found itself beached. Crow stuffed the hole full of rocks and the whale died; presenting Crow with another fine feast.

The Tanaina say that Crow eventually came to regret his mischievous tricks and decided to help people out. When one community complained to him that a selfish chief had stolen the sun and moon, Crow recaptured them in a series of adventures that recall Raven's brushes with the miser and Main's pursuit of the great elk (see pages 34–35).

A Forest Full of Tricksters

Raven and Crow are not the only culture heroes who use trickery and guile to help themselves or humankind. In the dark forests of the Arctic's vast wooded regions, hundreds of other animals compete for fortune and favour – among them the hare and the beaver.

The Netsilik Inuit of Canada say the hare created daylight by using a magically powerful form of words. In a verbal duel with the fox, who liked the dark, the hare triumphed because its words were stronger. But darkness followed after the light, ensuring that both animals were kept happy. The story echoes a version which features the raven and the peregrine (scc pages 34–35).

The people of Siberia recount a further form of the tale in which the stolen sun is recovered and released by the heroic hare. According to the Chukchi, when the wicked spirits that plague their land also took away the sun, the shivering people were rescued from the misery of a life in perpetual darkness by the Arctic hare.

One fateful summer the radiant sun disappeared because the *kelet*, spirits who brought harm to the peoples of the north, had stolen it. At that time the sun lived close to the Earth and it was easy for the *kelet* to bundle it up and hide it in

The sun hangs low over a thickly forested area of Siberia. Fear of a permanent loss of the sun is a frequent motif in Arctic myths in which various mammal trickster figures retrieve or rescue it.

their tent. The hunters gathered to bewail their fate when into their midst bounded the resourceful Hare, declaring that he would track the sun down and restore it to the sky.

Hare searched far and wide and at last he found the *kelet*'s tent. Seeing a golden glow from within he bounded onto the roof and looked down the smoke hole: there he saw the *kelet* playing with the golden globe as if it were a ball. Down he leaped into their midst, surprising them so much that they dropped the precious sun.

The greedy *kelet* looked on Hare as their dinner and crowded close around him – but he was crafty and more than a match for the spirits. He offered to bring them two bladder skins of seal oil for lighting, heating and food. While they discussed his offer, he kicked the sun upwards with one of his strong legs. It rose, reached the smoke hole but then fell back to the ground.

A great clamour arose among the spirits when they saw that the hare was trying to steal the sun, but he distracted them once more, this time by offering three skins of oil. While they thought this proposal over, he kicked the sun upwards again. This time the globe soared up through the hole and on into the heavens. Then Hare followed it, springing on his strong haunches out through the hole and away to where the *kelet* could not find him. The peoples of the north rejoiced to see the sun bring warmth to the skies again.

The Cunning Beaver-man

In many Alaskan and Canadian traditions, Beaver-man was also a great trickster. One winter he found a trap on the icy ground where a spear stuck up stained with blood. Crafty Beaver-man pretended to be caught in the trap in order to find out who had set it. It was not long before a giant, bushy-tailed wolverine came along and chuckled softly to find another animal impaled on the spear. Beaver-man played dead as the wolverine carried him home, but back at the wolverine's dwelling, Beaver-man sprang to life, killing the giant mother and father wolverine and their two enormous children. When he sliced open the mother, he found two pups inside her, about the size that fully grown wolverines are today. He freed them and told them not to grow any bigger. They should not eat people as their parents had done, he said, but gophers and rabbits instead. But the wolverines scampered away, laughing at him and he could not catch them to teach them a lesson.

When Beaver-man encountered a giant bear, the bear said he had a fine marriageable daughter and promised her to Beaver-man if he would kill a series of animals that were troubling him. In truth he wanted Beaver-man out of the way and he hoped that the animals would kill him.

First Beaver-man had to make himself a bow and arrow. He cut wood from a great redwood tree, took sinew for the string from a fierce grizzly bear that he had outwitted and killed, found paint to decorate the arrow, and plucked a feather to adorn it from a giant eagle. While fetching it he had to kill the parent eagles; as with the wolverines, he instructed their child not to grow any bigger and taught it not to eat human flesh.

Armed with his new weapon, Beaver-man returned to fight the bears. First he killed their daughter, then ran off down to the lake. He turned into beaver form and leaped into the water. The bears threw nets in to catch him but Beaver simply filled the nets with logs and pulled on them while the bears strained to lift them from the water. When he suddenly let go the bears fell into the water and he killed them with ease.

In an intriguing variant of this tale told by the Kaska, the place of the bear was taken by a giant cannibal who was the sun himself. After many competitions the cannibal finally accepted that Beaver was his superior and ascended to the sky. Beaver married the cannibal's twin daughters only to find that they were alone in the world because two ravens had driven all the game animals away and as a result all the humans had starved to death. Beaver tricked the ravens by pretending to be dead. When they saw his body they flew down to gorge themselves – and he grabbed their feet and thrust them into his campfire.

The Shaman's Quest

The Arctic shaman was a community's link with the spirit world. Becoming such a spiritual mediator, however, was far from easy. Every shaman had to go through an intense visionary initiation in the course of which he or she became associated with powerful helper spirits.

The Canadian Inuit told of a woman named Uvavnuk who discovered her destiny as a shaman one moonless night, only metres from her house. She had gone out alone to pass water and as she squatted down the sky above her suddenly lit up. She looked up to see a blazing meteor hurtling towards her – and before she could move the flaming rock had struck her unconscious. But in the instant before she passed out she was aware of a brilliant light that burned inside her, and she saw the spirit of the meteor take possession of her. It had two bodies joined – on one side a polar bear and on the other a human.

A few moments later Uvavnuk rose, filled with shamanic power. She skipped into her house singing over and over a wild, sweet song about how the Earth and its all-powerful elements had taken possession of her and filled her with joy. In the house she could see all secrets and in her trance was able to name all the sins and broken taboos of the members of her household; these the offending members quickly began to confess – and so Uvavnuk was able to purify them all.

The spirit passed, the fire seemed to leave Uvavnuk and she became an ordinary woman again. But it was to return many times in her life,

each time inspiring her to powerful shamanic acts. Shortly before her death she declared she had won a concession from the spirits on her shamanic voyages and would banish hunger from her people – and for an entire year after she died the villagers experienced unprecedented hunting success.

Uvavnuk's experience of a brilliant light within was common among novice shamans. It was often likened to a fire or to lightning. The essential quality that distinguished a shaman from ordinary mortals was called *angakua* among the Iglulik Inuit, and one form of *angakua* was this brilliant internal light, or *qaumaneq* ("Lightning").

Torn Limb from Limb

The polar bear spirit that features in Uvavnuk's story appears frequently in the initiations of Inuit shamans. They commonly have to endure a psychic dismemberment akin to being torn limb from limb and eaten alive by the spirit-bear. While their souls are enduring this violent initiation, their bodies lie as if lifeless in a coma, as in the Siberian story of the powerful Nganasan shaman, Dyukhade (see page 48).

An important phase of initiation was the acquisition of spirit helpers. They were often animal spirits and had similar qualities and attributes to the animals themselves: a bear spirit helper was fierce, a fish swift and capable of swimming underwater. Sometimes mountain spirits or human ghosts

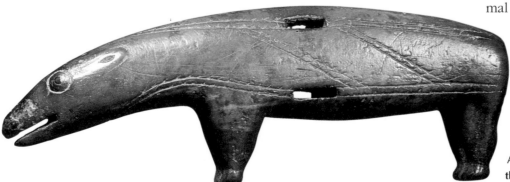

An Inuit ivory carving of a polar bear, one of the shaman's most powerful helper spirits.

offered themselves as helpers. Among the Copper Inuit, shamans believed in a boulder that they said existed in a land beyond daylight. This rock had the magical ability to sing, and shamans would make soul flights to it to enlist the help of its spirit.

In some traditions, shamans could give their spirit helpers bodily form. Among the Siberian Yakut, shamans would anoint the amulets that contained the power of their spirit helpers with the blood of reindeer and believed that this created living animals to voyage on their behalf to the world of the spirits.

Wooden carving, from Alaska, of a shaman in the grip of a trance. Two helper spirits, summoned by the drum, are shown at his side guiding him on his journey through hazardous realms.

According to the Iglulik, the spirit helpers usually came to the novice shaman after he or she had experienced violent dismemberment or a vision of the body as a bare skeleton (see box, page 89). Copper Inuit tradition held that the spirits were attracted to initiates when they saw them shining brightly with an inner light.

87

A late-19th-century Chukchi charm necklace or *okamak*, with male amulets of whalebone and a fur-wrapped female one known as "the mistress". These would protect the wearer from the many bad spirits that stalked the Earth.

It was traditional among the Mackenzie and Copper Inuit that when an established shaman was inducting an initiate, the teacher could sell the pupil one of his or her helper spirits. Sometimes, however, the helper spirits were passed on at death. The Copper Inuit told of a woman shaman named Higilak who was alone one day shortly after her father's death when she met his former helping spirits – they had come to be her helpers henceforth. In various traditions the helper spirits were bestowed upon shamans by the Wind Indweller or the Moon Man. Among the Caribou Inuit inexperienced shamans had to attract the attention of the Wind Indweller in order to win his favour and the gift of helper spirits.

The Spirits Come Near

Generally, a shaman's initiation began with an approach by the spirits. Often an individual had an initial desire to be a shaman, or *angakoq*, which drove him or her to look for the spirits in the deep silence of the countryside, far from any settlements. Uvavnuq was unusual in encountering her spirit close to home. A Polar Inuit shaman named Otaq encountered his spirits in the loneliness of the hills, where he had gone in the hope of being accepted as an *angakoq*. They towered over him, as tall as great tents, and sang songs. Twice he sought them out in the hills, and the second time

one of them spoke, asking him to carve them a ladle made of wood. The third time the spirits came to find him in his home, bringing at their heels a fleet-footed dog of many colours which also became a helper spirit. When the people of his village fell ill, Otaq tried his shamanic powers for the first time and found that they were great indeed. The people were all cured.

Sometimes the initiation took the form of a journey, as in the case of Aquppak, who went to live among the whales and returned a shaman (see page 77). The Alaskan story of Qipugaluatchiaq, the hunter who married a caribou, entered a new cycle after his animal wife returned to the wild; he felt the calling to be a shaman and travelled to the seabed on a voyage of initiation. There on the floor at the very centre of the ocean he came to an iglu from which a woman emerged. She said he had been summoned and ushered him inside. He met a whale-man who handed over a slice of his own whale-skin, from just under the jaw. He then told Qipugaluatchiaq to take the skin home and promised that if the shaman reached his village before it had shrunk away then the people there would soon be feasting on whale flesh.

Qipugaluatchiaq returned home a shaman. He brought the piece of skin safely to the village and the following day a great dead whale drifted in from the sea. Then, that winter, Qipugaluatchiaq was summoned to rescue his nephew Maguan who was stranded on a floating iceberg.

Maguan, close to death, was revived by the sound of his uncle's voice, but when he looked up saw a great white bear towering over him. There on the ice far from help Maguan assumed his days were at an end; but Qipugaluatchiaq lifted his nephew's body gently onto his back, taking care not to slice the youth's flesh with his bear claws, and carried him home again. Qipugaluatchiaq took the form of a bear because in exercising his shamanic power he had assumed the form and powers of his helper spirit. The bear was also the animal whose amulet Qipugaluatchiaq carried; an amulet which embodied the shaman's power to transform himself into a bear.

A legend from Greenland recounts how a shaman named Tugtutsiak held a seance at a time of famine, feeding the people being a common task for a shaman in times of poor or failed hunting (see page 86). First he summoned his polar bear and walrus helpers. Both animals could immediately be heard clamouring outside the house where the seance was being held. The bear seized the shaman and threw him bodily to the walrus, who passed him back to the bear. Between them the animals carried him far from his home village to a new and strange country that he understood was lower than the Earth. He found that he was at the bottom of the sea, where he was required to propitiate the Sea Mother for human sins and persuade her to release the sea mammals. When he had completed his mission successfully the animal spirits transported him home safely.

Another recurrent shamanic journey was to the moon (see box, page 90). In West Greenland the Kalaallit told of a man named Kanak who, seeking solitude one evening, found himself lifted to a country in the sky where he encountered Moon-man and underwent initiation as a shaman. Moon-man showed his house to Kanak, who had to step over a fierce dog in the entrance. Within, he showed Kanak a hole in the floor through which he could see all the lands of the north

Seeing Through the Skin

In some traditions it was a vital phase of shamanic initiation for the shaman to see him- or herself as a skeleton.

Among the Iglulik Inuit of Baffin Island, a developing shaman – usually a man – had to consolidate his supernatural powers by dispensing with his flesh and blood for the duration of an intense visionary period. Once he could see himself as a skeleton, he had to identify each bone of his body in the arcane language of the shaman. Anthropological fieldworkers found that the shamans were unable or unwilling to explain why and how they did this. Scholars interpret it as an act of self-dedication or consecration to the life of the shaman, using the least perishable aspect of the human body, the bones that far outlive the flesh.

The shaman's vision of himself as a skeleton is common in Siberia, too. It is part of the process by which every aspect of the shaman's being is made familiar to the helping spirits on which he will call when he is fully initiated. As on Baffin Island it is a vital part of the shaman's dedication to his calling.

The Inuit say that when shamans are actively negotiating with the spirit world they are often transparent. In evening sunlight the shaman can dissociate himself from his shadow, which trips away into the twilight. Then his body glows with the red light of the sun, allowing onlookers to magically see through his skin, revealing both his powerful spirit and the bones of his skeleton.

A 19th-century shaman's mask from the lower Kuskokwim River region in Alaska showing the body's skeleton.

Kukiaq and the Moon

One tale from the Netsilik Inuit of northeastern Canada told how a shaman was transported to the celestial realm, where he met the spirits of the sun and the moon.

One evening a shaman named Kukiaq was waiting patiently by a seal's breathing hole for the chance to spear one of the creatures. Land, sea and air were frozen, silent, and he looked with a steady gaze on the vast moon that hung in the sky.

As he stood watching the moon came nearer, sweeping through the night-sky until it loomed directly above him. It then took the form of a tall, stern-faced man on a sledge made from whale jawbones and pulled by dogs. At Moon-man's command Kukiaq sat on the sledge, closed his eyes and was swept away across the star-sprinkled sky.

Then he heard the sleigh crunch on new ice and opened his eyes to see a village crowded with people. He met two friends from the old days, long dead, and they clapped him on the shoulder in welcome: he knew he was in the celestial country of the dead, far above the Earth.

Moon-man showed the bright windows of his home to Kukiaq and invited him in. For a moment Kukiaq blanched: the walls of the entrance passage and of the house were moving in and out in a terrifying fashion. In the entrance itself lay a fierce dog. But Kukiaq knew that if he showed no fear he would be unharmed.

Inside he encountered a beautiful woman who sat peacefully nursing a child. At her side was a lamp turned so high that it scorched Kukiaq's neckband. This woman, Kukiaq understood, was the sun herself. She welcomed Kukiaq and made space for him on the bench at her side. Kukiaq longed to stay, but he was wise enough to know that if he sat with her once he would never find his way back to Earth.

He ran from Moon-man's house, and allowed himself to tumble earthwards. At the end of a long fall he found himself standing on the ice by the very same hole from which he had departed only moments earlier.

where men lived and hunted. Then he served him food, which was brought by a woman whose skeleton was visible through her back.

Moon-man warned Kanak that he would next meet a terrible old hag who would try to make him laugh – and if she succeeded she would rip his intestines out as her prize; if Kanak were tempted to smile, Moon-man said, he should dig his fingernails into his leg beneath the knee. Sure enough the old woman came in and cavorted ludicrously before Kanak, but he used his nails as instructed and then Moon-man stepped forward and shooed her away.

Moon-man also showed Kanak how he blew snow down to Earth through the hole in the floor. Finally he indicated that the time had come for Kanak to return to Earth; but he warned him that if he showed fear he would find himself dead, his soul swept away with no way back to the land of the living. As Moon-man lowered him through the hole in the floor Kanak fainted, but when consciousness returned he was safe on Earth. As his senses came slowly back, he heard the voice of his dead grandmother on the icy air and realized that her spirit had helped him return. Kanak became a renowned shaman.

Sometimes the prospective shaman was already an important figure such as a great seal- or bear-hunter; at others he or she was an outcast. In the story of the orphan boy (see page 103), a despised youth left home to wander in the mountains where he appealed to the spirits who gave him supernatural knowledge of animals and people and great powers as a hunter. A version of this tale, told in Labrador, had the boy call on the Moon-man for help. He appeared on Earth as a giant and dragged the boy off to a beach where he beat him with a whip. But the beating, like a shamanic initiation, gave the youth strength, and he emerged from the ordeal full of power.

A Yupik finger mask representing the moon. Made from wood and fringed with polar bear hair, it would have been worn by a woman during dance rituals.

According to another strand of the tradition, shamans were born and not made: a child in the family of a deceased shaman would inherit the gift. Sometimes such a child was recognized by the physical characteristics of their ancestor.

Detailed prohibitions governed the behaviour of shamans for as much as a year after initiation was deemed to be complete. Particular foods were banned – in coastal Alaska, food that belonged to the sea or beach was judged to repel the shamans' spirits and would cause them to depart. In other areas parts of animals – in particular, the head, guts or tongue – were taboo for the same reason. Women shamans were forbidden to sew or make clothes and boots – the primary duty of an Inuit wife.

The Heroic Shaman

The shaman, once initiated, had to prove his or her power by protecting the local people from a variety of misfortunes. Many myths and stories recount shamans' journeys to wondrous and dangerous realms where they endured heroic encounters with fierce spirits.

A story told by the Chukchi celebrated the encounter of a powerful shaman named Kykvat ("Dried Meat") with a *kele*, or evil spirit that was carrying a vicious disease throughout the region. Populations to the north of Kykvat's village had been decimated by the disease and the shaman's keen spirit vision revealed to him that the *kele* was stalking southwards and would soon be upon his people. He warned them that it would arrive that very night. He would waylay it, he announced, but they should stay awake and listen for his voice, and be prepared to come to help him if he called.

Some distance from the village Kykvat dug a hole in the snow and squatted in it to await the *kele*. He did not doubt his conviction that it would come and sure enough at midnight it arrived, riding over the crisp snow in a boat of animal skins pulled by a dog. The *kele* asked Kykvat what he was doing far from the village in the freezing night and the shaman declared that the villagers would not let him stay with them. At once the *kele* offered Kykvat shelter and food on condition he became his helper. Kykvat pretended to agree.

The *kele* put up a *yaranga*, or tent of animal skin, and sent Kykvat to choose some meat from the boat. He found it heavily weighed down with human corpses, and there were even some living people there, tightly bound with rope. There was also deer meat, so Kykvat secretly took a piece and returned to the *yaranga*. The *kele* asked about a renowned shaman named Kykvat whom he had heard lived in the area and Kykvat looked at him inquiringly, feigning ignorance. He told the spirit that the fellow was no longer known in the area and must have died some time ago. The *kele* was greatly relieved, and the shaman could see that he was frightened of the great Kykvat.

Then Kykvat went outside on the pretext of passing water. Beneath the sparkling stars he approached the *kele's* dog silently as a shadow and killed it. Then he cut loose the living people from the boat. He set them on their feet, slapped them on the rump like deer and told them to be gone to their homes. Some of the poor folk, however, were already as good as dead – for although their bodies were alive the evil spirit had eaten their souls; they fell to the ground comatose.

The spirit wondered what Kykvat was up to all this time and sent his wife out to investigate. Kykvat killed her, too, then raced into the *yaranga*, leaped on the *kele* and pinned him to the ground. With a great roar he called to the villagers, who came armed with spears and ropes. They bound the *kele* tightly and forced his mouth wide open. Shaman and people poured slop water into the monster's mouth for long months, from spring through an entire summer – and only in the autumn did the liquid finally fill his gargantuan belly. Then the foul-smelling water spilled down the evil spirit's sharp chin. Kykvat's triumph was complete. He made the *kele* promise never to return to the region before setting the thing free.

Flights of Rescue

Of course, the shaman was not able to keep the community entirely free of disease. When sickness did strike he or she would be called upon to undertake a soul voyage to rescue a particular patient from the grip of disease or even death. Many stories celebrate these fearless missions.

The Reindeer Chukchi tell of a female shaman who used her great powers to bring her son back to life. The woman was not at home when the boy died, for she had gone to the land across the sea, beyond the boundaries of this world, to help another family whose son was close to death. When she arrived there that boy had died, but she held a long seance, drummed powerfully, found his soul and reclaimed him from death's grasp. As a reward she was given two teams of reindeer, one spotted black and one spotted white. The woman remained with his people for a full twelve months.

When she returned home, she found that her own son had died while she was away. She went in to the house to rest, but her husband – who was in a frenzy of rage because she had been away when she was sorely needed – would not let her sleep and insisted that she shamanize and save her boy at once. So she embarked on a soul flight to the bottom of the sea but she could not find him there.

Then she took one of the reindeer teams she had brought home from the otherworldly land and set off high into the sky. There she first encountered a glossy black raven who said how much he liked the team, then a great eagle who also expressed his admiration for it. She offered the eagle the other reindeer team, the one she had left at her husband's house, and in exchange he told her that her son's soul was in the custody of a foul-breathed monster.

The shaman's next stop was the monster's house, where she found her son tied to a pole and the monster away on business. She escaped with him, but the monster, returning soon afterwards, gave chase. The shaman called on all her helper spirits but only two diver birds came to her aid. One of the birds then told her to watch the sky: if it reddened, it meant the helper spirits had slain the monster. Shortly after the divers flitted away the sky did indeed glow blood-red.

The shaman landed safely among her people and summoned them to a seance. They brought out her son's body and placed it among them as she began drumming. She then saw the raven and the eagle come and take up position on either side of the corpse. As the crowd watched, the skin on the corpse's limbs became fresh once more. In ringing tones the mother called on her son to wake. As the sun rose, he came back to life. The shaman ordered both reindeer teams to be slaughtered; she intended them as gifts for the raven and eagle who had helped her.

The contrast of colours on this Chukchi shaman's hat, c.1880, symbolizes the visionary's dual role in the world of spirits and people.

The Healing Power of Reindeer

Reindeer held a privileged position in the traditions and mythology of Arctic Siberia. The Even revered reindeer as a gift from the gods; Even shamans often kept a white or piebald deer as a special helper known as a *kuj-jai*. The *kujjai* was used in healing rituals; in very serious cases it took on the spirit of a disease to save a patient. In these cases the *kujjai* was set free and allowed to roam until its death.

A myth from Greenland tells of a shaman named Aalisa who travelled to the moon to rescue his missing daughter. When he landed there he discovered a house and within it he encountered Moon-man hard at work cutting flakes from a walrus tusk. Aalisa wondered silently what the man was doing and Moon-man must have read his thoughts because he answered aloud that he was making snowflakes to fall on the Earth far below.

Then Aalisa saw his daughter sitting with two other women on the hut's sleeping platform. They were as pale as ghosts, and Moon-man explained that they had had their bowels removed by Erlaveersinioq the Disemboweller who came to dance before all newcomers to the moon.

This fearsome individual was a familiar figure in tales of shamanic flights to the moon and of contests with vision-monsters. She took different names in different regions and used various means to try to make her victims laugh, in some cases

An Inuit shaman's belt from northeast Canada. The sounds made by the bells when the wearer moved would attract the spirits.

exposing herself and cavorting wildly, in others singing wheedling nonsense songs. Kanak, among others, had to endure her attentions (see page 89). Usually Moon-man warned visitors what to do if they felt they could not hold back their laughter. Kanak was told to dig his nails into his leg to stop himself; in another version – one of many variants in which the visitor to the moon is an abused wife who appeals to the moon and is swept up to Moon-man's dwelling – the woman is told to make the shape of a polar bear with her hands and issue bear noises to keep the Disemboweller at bay.

Moon-man informed Aalisa that he too would be tempted by Erlaveersinioq; if he did not laugh and so passed the test, he would have his daughter to take back to Earth. Aalisa looked up – and in came Erlaveersinioq at once. She began to caper about with a knife and an old plate, from time to time crowing in triumph and claiming that Aalisa's countenance was at last cracking into a smile. But all the while Aalisa kept a perfectly straight face. Finally Erlaveersinioq admitted defeat. The great shaman's daughter was restored to life and he took her home.

In Times of Storm and Famine

The shaman's role in preserving the community's well-being extended to maintaining a good supply of game for hunters on sea or land. When hunting was poor because of weather conditions or because the game animals had withdrawn their co-operation, Arctic peoples believed it to be the result of misbehaviour in the community – usually the breaking of one or more of the many taboos surrounding hunting and day-to-day behaviour. Then it was up to the shaman to undo this wrong and set things right.

Many Inuit peoples living on the coast believed that the weather was bad or the hunting poor because they had angered the Sea Mother or Mistress of the Sea Mammals (see page 96), variously called Sedna, Takanakapsaluk or Nuliajuk. They expected the shaman to prevail upon her to forgive them and restore the supply of animals she controlled. Usually the shaman made a journey to the seabed to confront the Sea Mother in her lair.

The shaman encountered many dangers on this quest. First he would call the villagers together for a seance; he concealed himself behind a curtain while they occupied the main part of the room. While they sang songs of spiritual support, the shaman descended to the seabed. His first test there was to pass skilfully between three vast rolling stones that banged together and threatened to crush him to death. Then he followed a path

Defeating Evil Spirits

Smallpox was once a great killer in Siberia. But the shamans of the Even people believed that the spirit of the disease was visible – and when they saw it they challenged it to single combat.

When migrating reindeer herders arrived in an Even settlement they would sometimes bring smallpox with them. The disease was thought to take the form of a red-headed Russian woman sitting on a sledge towards the rear of the long caravan, invisible to all but the local shaman. As the villagers greeted the newcomers and examined their herds, the shaman eyed them warily. If the shaman saw the dreaded visitor, he or she would warn the people and prepare to repulse the spirit.

The woman was a strong spirit indeed and often two or three shamans had to pool their strength to take her on. They would call a special seance and the people would gather to help out.

When the smallpox attacked she became a stamping red bull that charged head down at the shaman. If the shaman failed the consequences were grim: he and all the local people would die, save two of the shaman's family who would be left alive to bury the dead. But if the disease spirit was vanquished, it had to go on its way unsatisfied and smallpox hurt no one in the encampment.

A Siberian shaman holds up the drum he used to summon spirits he would either negotiate with or fight.

that looked like a coastline on the Earth's surface and led to a vast underwater plain where he found Takanakapsaluk's house. In the passage before the house lay a snarling dog, but if the shaman stepped fearlessly over it – like Kanak and Kukiaq on their moon visits (see pages 89–91) – then it was pacified.

Sometimes the shaman found a tall wall surrounding Takanakapsaluk's compound. This indicated that she had taken particular offence with the people. Then the shaman used all his bodily strength to knock it down, throwing himself against the hard bricks and taking many knocks. Within the house he found Takanakapsaluk sitting beside a lamp and a great pool filled with all the seals, walruses and whales that the people on Earth were so sorely missing. She had her back to the pool. Her hair was tangled and knotted with human sins, which also formed a cloud of foul fog that hung around her. Her matted hair hung down over her eyes and because she had lost her fingers (see pages 58–59) she could not clean or untangle it.

Approaching across the room, the shaman had to be wary of Takanakapsaluk's father Isarrataitsoq – who would try to seize the intruder, assuming him or her to be a soul come to seek pardon for its sins. As he lunged the shaman had to cry out that he was flesh and blood and the old man would at once back away. Then the shaman gently took hold of Takanakapsaluk, turned her towards the lamp and the pool and combed and cleaned her hair for her.

Appeasing Takanakapsaluk was a major task. As the shaman soothed her, she named the many breaches of taboo and other sins committed by the people of his village. If his mission was successful, however, she would eventually relent. Taking the sea creatures from the pool beside her lamp, she would throw them on the floor, where a whirlpool appeared and swept them back to sea. The period of want was finally over.

Then the shaman sped back to the surface of the Earth. The villagers who had gathered for the seance heard him return, making seal-like noises. They then began to confess the taboos they had broken and the sins they had committed. Sometimes it was necessary to call for someone who had broken a minor taboo and who was not present, and he or she would be brought into the seance to make a public confession. Finally all wrongdoing was named and laid to rest. Prosperity was now assured.

Appeasing the Mother of the Sea

The tradition of shamanic propitiation of the Sea Mother is found among Inuit peoples in coastal regions over a very wide area, from eastern Greenland to the western regions of Canada – and there are many variants. In some regions the shaman, rather than descending personally to the seabed, sent his helper spirits to ask the Sea Mother what had offended her. In other areas, the shaman sent down a rope with a hook on its end, and pulled the Sea Mother along a hidden passage to a place just outside or beneath the site of the seance; the shaman then made the Sea Mother promise to restore the animals before he or she allowed her to go back to her home.

Among the Netsilik, Takanakapsaluk was named Nuliajuk, Isarrataitsoq was a woman and they both shared a sea scorpion as their husband. As well as a dog, an *inua* stood guard over the house and he kept careful record of all the people's violations of taboo; scholars have identified in this an echo of the Christian vision of Saint Peter, who is said to guard the Gates of Heaven. Nuliajuk was said to have a child named Ungaq ("One Who Screams"), who had been stolen from a sleeping mother on Earth.

The shaman often performed this task on behalf of the whole community but sometimes did it for a single individual who had endured a long lean period in the hunt or who had serious illness in the family and who feared that the Sea Mother was pursuing a personal vendetta.

Trickster Shamans

Such was the enormous power and influence available to the shaman that it was perhaps inevitable that not all of them harnessed their energies to positive ends. Rivalry commonly developed between shamans who were competing for the attention of the people among whom they lived, and shamans were often drawn into competition and confrontation with each other. Some shamans were able to create vicious spirit beings to attack their enemies; the shamans made effigies named *tupilaq* from animal skins and parts of human bodies for the spirits to ride and then sent them to bring an enemy to ruin.

Tupilaq were often made in the shape of seals, and it was believed that such effigies could magically turn into real seals. These animals were dangerous, since any hunter who happened to kill a *tupilaq* seal without realizing what it was would die. The story of such an unlucky hunter – named Tateraq – was told by the Polar Inuit. Tateraq showed great skill in dispatching a seal one day in autumn, but he was overtaken by horror when he and his hunting friends cut it open – for they discovered the chest bone of a human corpse and bones from various other animals. They knew at once it was a *tupilaq*. Within months the man was ill and sliding slowly to a lonely death, remembering with agony his life as a hunter. Shamans were also said to use spells and conjuration to steal the souls of men, who also died.

In an episode recounted in Tikigaq a shaman named Atanauraq sent a *tupilaq* seal to harm two brothers, Kiligvak and Suuyuk, when they went out seal-hunting on the ice. The *tupilaq* targeted Kiligvak first, but he was saved by a wolf's-snout amulet that he was carrying. Kiligvak saw the seal and felt a great warmth in his belly – this warned him not to attack, because a man who felt such a glow was under attack from a shaman. He chewed the amulet to make it more powerful, then rubbed his belly with it, repelling Atanauraq's black magic. Suuyuk, however, was not so wise. When the *tupilaq* approached him, thrashing about in the water to attract his attention, the man shot at it, leaped up eagerly to fetch the carcass and then felt a burning in his stomach. He spat and saw blood pouring from his mouth. He soon died – and all because Atanauraq used his shamanic power for an evil purpose.

A *tupilaq* from East Greenland. Such hideous figures were made by shamans and brought to life in order to bring harm to other people.

IN THE REALM OF THE SPIRITS

Shamans negotiated with spirits to effect change and reconciliation in the material world, be it to heal the sick, ensure a successful hunt or seek justice from a wrong-doer. Their world, however, could be violent and terrifying, and it was invariably disturbing.

When shamans awoke from their trances it seemed to some as if they had returned from the dead. And yet it was not the shaman's physical self which undertook these journeys. By donning a mask, he or she would assume a spiritual self that would face the dangers of the spirit world and seek the resolution that the community desired. The ritual that surrounded this journey was not understood just as a dramatic performance. To the shamans and their followers it was terrifyingly real.

Above: A figure of a spirit, known as a *tupilaq*, which would be brought to life by a shaman during his journey into the spirit world. These usually grotesque objects could be used to bring harm to other rival shamans.

Below: An Inuit shaman, in a trance, embarking on a journey to battle with spirits. He is bound with rope to prevent his spirit helpers from flying away.

Right: A shaman's soul would depart from its body and travel the other world to confront influential spirits. Such a journey is depicted by this Alaskan mask, which has an image of the shaman's soul in the centre.

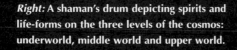

Right: A shaman's drum depicting spirits and life-forms on the three levels of the cosmos: underworld, middle world and upper world.

Below right: A wooden doll from Cook Inlet, Alaska, used by a Tanaina shaman to help cure illness. It is wearing a "rich man's belt", a symbol of wealth and prestige. The Tanaina believed that such dolls had lives of their own.

RITUAL AND THE BONDS OF COMMUNITY

The inhabitants of the Tikigaq peninsula in northwestern Alaska had always lived by whaling. Looking at the low hump of land which was their home, they even saw a resemblance to a whale, and their myths described how one of the great sea creatures had been transformed into solid ground after being harpooned by Raven, their legendary progenitor (see page 78). But their concern with the hunt went deep into their mental landscape also. Throughout the year they observed an elaborate series of festivities, taboos and ceremonies, all of them directed at propitiating the whales and ensuring that they would return in future years. The songs people sang, the dances they performed, the stories they told, the adornments they wore – all revolved around the whale hunt and the struggle for subsistence it represented.

Living in one of the world's most extreme environments, the inhabitants of the far north had no choice but to co-operate with nature in order to survive. Yet the limited resources available never permitted the foundation of large settlements; there were no Arctic cities. Instead, they resided in small, tight-knit communities, usually based around extended families. People moved in tiny groups over enormous distances. Everyone knew one another and memories were long.

It was also a place where periods of intense effort alternated with long spells of relative inactivity. In particular the long polar winter left whole communities with time on their hands. Taking advantage of this opportunity, many northerners developed an elaborate round of ceremonial in which the founding myths of each society were acted out. Music, dance and story-telling all played a part in bringing the community together and reaffirming its beliefs, hopes and fears.

Myth also expressed itself in the very structure of northern society – in the relations between the sexes, in attitudes towards the community and in the final mystery of death. Even today, when Christianity has largely supplanted traditional beliefs and children go to school to learn about the wider world, indigenous Arctic societies are unusually self-contained. In the past, when they were literally cut off from the rest of humankind, they formed worlds in miniature whose traditional beliefs shaped the way their inhabitants ate, slept and breathed.

Opposite: Nenets reindeer herders in Yamal, Siberia. Such peoples came together by necessity, but were bound by complex ritual and kinship ties.

Below: The belief in harmonizing spirit and matter, ritual and utility, is reflected in this Inuit comb, the shape of which honours its whalebone material.

A Society Based on Sharing

The northern peoples were forced together by the harsh environment, which made co-operation and a concern for others necessities. A rich seam of legend described the dangers of solitude and the need to act unselfishly if the community as a whole was to thrive.

The northern world in general, and Inuit society in particular, was a place of small communities often isolated from one another by difficult terrain and substantial distances. The majority of people lived in small hamlets, typically with fewer than fifty inhabitants; only in such resource-rich regions as the southwest Alaskan coast were there large villages with several hundred people in them. In many areas there were no villages at all, only nomads' tents.

The result was that social life for most people was restricted to contact with their own kin. Often all the residents of a community would be related to one another. Given that communication with neighbouring settlements was usually difficult, interaction within the community was often intense. It was vital for the residents to get on with one another to avoid social breakdown or even outbreaks of violence.

One result of this need for social cohesion was an extraordinary number of rules and taboos, which determined correct behaviour in almost every situation down to the minutest detail. Besides ensuring that the spirits were not offended this concern with the right deportment had the side-effect of smoothing out most areas of social friction and of lowering stress levels in an environment where they might otherwise be very high.

Another effect was an extraordinary generosity that was simply taken for granted. Hunters who had had a successful trip were expected to share their good fortune with the rest of the community. As soon as news of their return spread, people would make their way to their houses carrying containers for cuts of meat that they considered theirs by right, and they would almost never be turned away empty-handed. The sharing out of game was an acceptance that ownership of nature's bounty was never exclusive. In this way even people too weak to go out hunting were supported as long as there was food to be had.

There was a particular concern with feeding the old, who were respected not just for their experience of traditional lore but also as founts of shamanic power. Treating the elderly rudely or failing to support them when they needed help were misdeeds that risked immediate retribution from the spirits; offenders were told that their limbs would swell up or they would find themselves marooned on some thin stretch of ice.

While men often hunted in solitude, feasting was a communal event with all members of a village sharing in the bounty of the hunt. Food was often served in bowls such as this bentwood dish, the painted mythological figure providing the starting point for tales told while everyone ate.

102

Sacrifices for the Next Generation

Starvation was a constant threat in the Arctic. When it loomed, the old and weak would sometimes voluntarily give up their own lives for the good of the community as a whole.

Outside observers have often remarked on the care and affection lavished on infants and old people in Inuit society. But in past times when famine was an ever-present danger, situations arose in which there was simply not enough food to feed a whole family or village. At such bitter moments it was not unknown for an elderly person to venture out into the wilderness to certain death in order to relieve the pressure on other family members.

Alternatively, someone who was very ill or an invalid might agree to be left behind when the group moved camp, on the grounds that he or she was anyway unlikely to survive the long and arduous journey and they would only slow them up dangerously as they went. The survivors accepted their deaths stoically, believing that the sacrifice was only temporary; the dead person would soon be back in spirit, for the next baby born into the community would be sure to receive his or her name (see page 118), a powerful cypher which would embody their spirit. Similar sacrifices were made by the peoples of Siberia.

A Nenets mother and her baby inside their reindeer-skin tent in Yamal, Siberia. Harsh conditions often required stark moral choices to preserve the younger generation.

The same social concern showed through in the treatment of children who had lost their parents. They were usually adopted by relatives who raised them as their own, ensuring that no one was left outside the tight social circle. Even so, their plight exerted a powerful hold on the Inuit imagination, for in a society dominated by family ties anyone without immediate kin seemed doubly bereft. The poor orphan struggling to survive in a hostile world became a stock figure in folktales.

One story, from the Mackenzie Delta region, described just such a boy who lived alone with his grandmother and was regularly mistreated by the other people in the village. As a result he got used to keeping his own company. Even when the villagers built a communal house where the men gathered most evenings, he rarely entered it, preferring to spend his time wandering alone outside.

103

One evening he roamed further than usual from the village, and eventually saw a bright light shining in the distance. Approaching, he found that it was another communal house, one he had never seen before. He looked in through the window, and almost at once heard a voice calling out, inviting him inside. He went in and found the building crowded with men, who were seated all around the walls.

Naturally enough the inmates were curious to know who the newcomer might be, and they repeatedly asked him if he was a shaman – for who else would be roaming the night alone? He denied it, until one of the men – displaying genuinely shamanistic insight – described his case to him exactly: he was just a poor orphan whom everyone mistreated, wandering far from home.

Sitting down cross-legged in the centre of the floor, the man then proceeded to give a spectacular demonstration of what a true shaman could do. Singing to himself in a low monotone, he seemed to drift off into a trance, lulling his audience into a semi-hypnotic state at the same time. Then, as the boy looked on in amazement, the floor of the building became misty and insubstantial, turning into an ice pool through which before long a seal poked its head. The shaman was waiting with a lance; and when he had duly speared and flensed the animal, he distributed its meat and skin to the assembled company.

He went on to work his magic twice more, once producing a netful of plump whitefish and the other time spiriting up a full-sized caribou, which he killed and divided among the watchers in the same way as he had done with the seal. By that time it was almost daylight, and the boy decided he ought to get back home. But as he set off across the snow he began brooding on what he

Playing games was another key feature of Arctic communal life. These two pieces of seal bone and a skin thong comprise the game of *ajagak* in which the player must attempt to catch one part of the toy in the other.

had seen. The shaman's deeds were truly miraculous but also seemed to hold a deep significance for the boy – for they had suggested to him a way to give his own sorry life meaning.

For some time he prepared himself spiritually, concentrating on the rituals observed by the shaman he had seen in that strange hut. Then one evening he put in an appearance at the communal house in his own village. He was so rarely seen there that his presence caused something of a stir, and it was not long before someone shouted across to him to take his turn at singing. Still unsure of the powers he had been perfecting, the boy determined nonetheless to put them to the test there and then. So he went to the centre of the floor, chanting the song the shaman had sung and repeating the words he had regularly intoned: "Spirit, help me". Then, as the audience gaped, the floor turned into an ice pool, just as it had before.

The orphan went on to repeat all his mentor's feats, for he himself had now become a shaman. From that time forth no one in the village ever treated him with anything but profound respect, for in discovering his latent abilities he had also found a social role.

A Communal Life

It was important to have a recognized place in Inuit society, for life was lived out very much on the public stage. Western concepts of privacy simply did not exist. Entire extended families would share one dwelling, with no more than a caribou-hide blanket separating the husband and wife from the rest of the household. Many bodies would huddle up for warmth on the communal sleeping platforms. In eastern Greenland the concept of sharing even extended as far as group sex; at celebrations or when guests visited, there was a custom called "putting out the lamp", in which the hosts would do just that, leaving the various couples to grope about in search of different sexual partners in the dark.

Inuit sociability also expressed itself in a passion for games of all kinds. In a world with few other recreational possibilities, these helped keep people occupied at times of the year when there was little else to do, relieving the stress that boredom and a claustrophobic social life might otherwise have engendered.

Children enjoyed such traditional amusements as juggling, skipping and spinning tops, as well as *ajagak*, their own version of the cup-and-ball game familiar in many parts of the world. In the Arctic it was normally played with the shoulder-blade of some small animal in which several holes had been drilled. The aim of the game was to throw the bone upwards and catch it on its descent by sticking an attached spike through one of the cavities, the smallest scoring highest.

For adults, sports provided exercise when there was little opportunity for hunting. Some, like football and wrestling, were local versions of worldwide favourites, but others had a distinctively northern flavour. The tug-of-war, using leather thongs for a rope, was particularly popular. So was blanket-tossing, an Alaskan equivalent of trampolining in which practitioners would fly as high as ten metres in the air, executing twists and somersaults along the way. This game is said to have originated in an attempt to spot whales out at sea from a flat coast.

The most competitive sporting contests were associated with the communal houses in the larger villages, which organized inter-house challenges in the winter months. The events might include foot races and wrestling as well as a variety of jumping contests tailored for indoor competition. One of the most spectacular was the two-legged high kick, in which contestants leaped to strike with both feet an object suspended from the ceiling. Men could often hit targets nearly three metres from the floor, with the women only about half a metre lower. Many of these sports are still popular today.

Wild Men of the Mountains

In this companionable world of extended families and communal assemblies, solitary beings were regarded as oddities to be feared. Mothers in Greenland would scare their children with tales of the *qivittut*, men who, often as a result of disappointment in love, had decided to leave their

An Asiatic Eskimo puppet made of driftwood and sealskin, with eyes of trade beads. This was a child's toy, but it may also have been used to stage humorous performances as entertainments.

The vegetation of the summer tundra in Yamal, Siberia, provided plenty of rich grazing for reindeer. This led, in recent centuries, to their domestication and the formation of herding.

villages and live alone in the mountains. They were thought of as wild men who, having spurned the spiritual warmth of human society, began gradually to turn into the animals whose company they shared; their hair grew long and matted, their bodies became covered in fur and their finger- and toe-nails grew untrimmed into claws. They lived in caves, and in winter, when they became haunted by their memories of human companionship, they would come down to the villages to steal food. They could sometimes be glimpsed peering hungrily in through windows, envious of the warmth and company inside.

They inspired many hunters' tales, too. Men back from expeditions in pursuit of polar bears or walruses would regale the village with stories of

how they had discovered mysterious human footprints outside their tents when they woke up in the morning, heading back towards the mountains. If dogs were found missing or dead, it was generally the *qivittut* who would get the blame.

For the rest of society, however, human companionship was as important as heat and light. Nor was it just the Inuit who regarded sharing as a duty. Helping out those who needed it was a fundamental value for all the peoples of the Arctic world, embraced across the Bering Strait in Siberia

as well as in North America and Greenland, as a story from the Even (Lamut) people of the Kolyma River region, in northeast Siberia, shows.

The Mean Herder

It tells of a wealthy herder, the owner of many reindeer. Such a man should have shared his good fortune with others, but this particular individual, egged on by a wife who was as avaricious as he was, begrudged giving even scraps of offal to the poor families in the camps where he stayed. His selfishness went unpunished until one day he refused to give food to an old shaman with magical powers. The wonder-worker went off muttering imprecations, and the next day the rich man woke up to find that his entire herd, the source of all his wealth, had disappeared. Only wolf tracks in the snow were to be seen where the sleek and well-fed deer had been resting the previous night.

Distraught, the man set off with his sons to find the missing creatures, but before long a blizzard blew up, obliterating the animals' tracks. There was no game to be found in the forest, and soon starvation loomed. In despair, the old man sank to his knees and cried out aloud for help.

He was answered by the Master of the Forest, the presiding spirit of Siberian animals. The spirit listened carefully as the old man recounted his woes. Then the Master promised to come to his aid – but not before letting him know that he had brought all these troubles on himself. For had he not forgotten the ancient custom of the Even peoples – always to give food to a poor neighbour who had none?

The delighted reindeer herder was effusive in his thanks, and with the spirit's guidance he and his sons soon found their way home. Nor was that the end of their good fortune, for the next morning the family woke to find that a large herd of wild reindeer had come to their camp overnight and were grazing peacefully around their home. Gratefully, they realized that that too must have been the Master of the Forest's doing.

From that time on the family had all the food they could ever want. But despite this lucky life of ease and abundance it soon became clear that they had not learned their lesson. The next time they made camp with other herders, the husband unwillingly prepared to distribute some poor scraps of food to those who had none. But his wife would have none of it; it would be better, she said, simply to move on.

Their selfishness, however, did not go unnoticed. The next morning their reindeer were gone again, and this time the Master of the Forest, who had taken away only what he had originally bestowed, would not answer their prayers. They went back to the camp they had left, but the other herders also refused to help them in their hour of need, knowing that they had done the same to others when they had been hungry. And so they slowly starved to death, and all as a punishment for their own meanness.

A knife for cutting packed snow, from Alaska, *c*.19th century. The etched scene, depicting caribou being driven towards a hunter, reflects the belief that the bounty of nature gave itself up to hunters as a gift. Failure to share it could lead to punishment, as the mean herder learned to his cost.

The Season of Ceremony

In the Inuit world, people's hopes, fears and deepest beliefs found expression in an annual round of ritual and ceremony whose purpose never strayed far from one overriding concern: guaranteeing good hunting.

The time for festivities ran from late November to January, when no sun at all is visible above the Arctic Circle. It was also the time when long-distance sledge travel became easy across the frozen land and sea, allowing large groups of people to meet up and celebrate.

Among the Inuit there was a noticeable geographical split between eastern and western communities. In Greenland the winter gatherings were for the most part relatively informal affairs, held whenever people came together in large numbers and food supplies allowed. There would be feasting, dances, songs, games, trade and shamanistic displays. In recent times Christmas has provided a focus for much of the socializing, and older, pagan traditions of house visits and gift-giving have become attached to it. In many villages it remains usual for the members of every household to call on one another during the festive period.

Some communities even now retain a more obvious remnant of pagan times in the rite known in Greenland as Mitaartut which also has equivalents among many Alaskan groups. Mitaartut is an odd composite of influences, mixing Danish mumming rites with native Inuit tradition; to southerners, it brings to mind Halloween and ancient memories of the Lord of Misrule.

For in Mitaartut, everything is topsy-turvy. Men dress as women, women as men – sometimes with a huge phallus added to emphasize the sexual identification. Faces may be blacked up with soot. The aim is to conceal a person's normal identity, for *mitaartut* means "people in disguise". Some may also put stockings or tie string across their face to give it a grotesque distortion.

Suitably concealed, sometimes under grotesque masks, the revellers roam the villages over a three-day period between Christmas and Twelfth Night. They go from house to house, rapping on doors, then entering to demand gifts.

The sledge, either reindeer- or dog-drawn, was essential for Arctic land travel, enabling hunting and trapping throughout the winter, as well as providing the means for disparate communities to come together for their ceremonials. Designs differed to suit the weather conditions, terrain and purpose. This Inupiat example was collected by John Ross in 1818.

Faces of Magical Significance

One key feature of Arctic ritual and ceremony was the wearing of masks, props which emphasized the gulf between appearance and inner reality, opening windows into the spirit world.

Masks were a regular feature of rituals and festivities in all parts of the Inuit world. In southern Alaska they were traditionally made of wood, while further north and in the eastern Arctic the materials were usually seal- or caribou skin.

Generally the masks were made by shamans, who infused them with something of their own spiritual power. They were painted with various natural dyes including soot, mineral deposits, berry juice and blood, and were often extravagantly decorated with tassels, feathers and other appendages, many of which had magical significance for the wearer.

Sometimes masks also served to adorn inanimate objects. In Tikigaq the whalers put a mask they called *inugluk* – "strange person" – on the largest of the three sealskin floats which were attached to each of their harpoons. Local shamans said that once the hunters had struck a target, the mask sang up from the depths to tell the crew where the diving whale was heading.

This 19th-century Yupik mask from the lower Yukon River region bears a grotesque face with handprints. The dots represent the stars in the night sky and the two limb appendages their spiritual form.

As the bizarre figures make their way in, speaking only in nonsense syllables, giggling children run for safety to their parents. The adults will jokingly quiz the visitors – maybe they are foreigners, perhaps even bogeymen from myth? The atmosphere is excited and amicable, with just a hint of real tension, and the encounters end in an offer of cakes or sweets. In exchange the masquers perform a grotesque dance and then take their leave to head on to their next destination.

In the western Arctic the celebrations can be altogether more elaborate. The Yupik of southwest Alaska were long renowned for the Bladder Festival, which was traditionally held annually over a period of weeks between November and January. The actual floating of the seal bladders from which it took its name came at the end of a lengthy ceremonial round that got under way several weeks earlier with the cleaning out of the communal house – rarely used at other times of year – and the composition of new songs for the coming festivities. Then there was the festival of Qaami'taaq, a fun time for the children when naked boys, their bodies elaborately painted, would noisily tour the village, carrying bowls to receive food gifts from the womenfolk, who sat at home waiting.

When Qaami'taaq finished it was time for Qengarpak, the Big Nose Festival, an Alaskan equivalent of Mitaartut in which the participants wore wooden masks and disguised themselves by wearing face paint and other people's clothes. Next in line was Aaniq, "Mothering", a custom continuing the theme of disguise and inverted social roles in which two men referred to as "mothers" would lead a group of boys, termed "dogs", on a ritual circle of the community, once more collecting gifts of food. Like huskies fighting for food scraps, the "dogs" would try and get at the pickings on the way back to the houses amid general noise and merriment.

The Bladder Festival itself stretched over as many as fifteen days. It began with the bladders of all the seals and walruses caught in the past season being taken back to the men's house, to be greeted with feasting and dancing. They were then inflated and hung from the rafters.

From this point on a whole range of taboos and ritual requirements came into play, all designed to avoid giving offence to the seals' souls, which were thought to be contained in the bladders. There had to be someone in the house constantly, and a lamp kept alight. Loud noises were forbidden, and sharp implements could not be used, bringing all work to an end. Sexual activity was also banned.

A round of social activities followed. One night the women would dance, performing special, slow improvisations said to imitate the mating of loons. Another night it was the turn of the young men. On a third evening there were public work-outs in which the young hunters would strive to outdo each other in feats of strength or agility.

Then, on the penultimate day of the festival, men would go down to the sea ice not far from the village and cut holes in it. That evening the entire village would gather in the men's house for a general giving of gifts; guests from neighbouring communities would also be invited. There would be singing and dancing all night long. At dawn

This hunter's drag handle is deeply symbolic; the main body of the tool represents a seal rising up through the water to breathe, while the top consists of a smaller seal which has broken the surface to investigate.

the bladders would be taken to the shore, where they were returned to their underwater home. To help them on their way, they were offered gifts including miniature paddles and tiny spearheads, designed to help the reincarnated animals with their own hunting.

There was an extensive lore associated with the Bladder Festival, the roots of which lay deep within Yupik mythology. The rite had its origins, the stories claimed, in the knowledge gained by a boy who had been sent by a powerful shaman to spend a year in the company of the seals, learning their ways and understanding their mentality. Eventually he was struck by a harpooner and taken back to the village in seal form. When the bladders of his companion seals had been returned to the sea, he reverted to his human shape and was found, naked and shivering, by a hole in the ice, crying because he could not go with the others. From him, the village learned how to treat the animals in the way they wished, so ensuring their goodwill and striking up a bond of consent between hunter and hunted.

The Lost Children

Even apparently small details of the rituals could have mythological significance, as a tale involving the painting of the children for the Qaami'taaq celebration recounts. It tells of the terrible fate of a group of youngsters who went out unprotected by the charcoal and white clay designs traditionally drawn on their bodies. They disappeared into the earth and found themselves lost underground. For days the villagers could hear them crying out in fear, but no one knew where the cries were coming from and they could do nothing to help. Eventually silence fell and most were never seen again.

A few, however, did return. They had made their way under the earth to the inside of a cliff-face not far from the village. There they closed their eyes and took five steps – the number in Inuit mythology traditionally separating the world of the dead from the living. Suddenly the cliff-face opened and they stumbled out into the light, among their own kind once more.

The Midwinter Sitting

An equally elaborate ritual cycle was played out on the Tikigaq peninsula, 1,000 kilometres further north up the Alaskan coast. Over the centuries an annual round of celebrations developed that reflected the inhabitants' unending concern with whale-hunting. The climax came in the midwinter ritual known as the Sitting. For four days boat-owners would sit in the communal houses thinking through the coming whaling season and the catches they would make. Meanwhile all work stopped in the village.

Their vigil was interspersed at regular intervals by a sequence of rites, evolved over generations. On the first day, for instance, scenes from the whale-hunt would be painted on the hut walls, while on the second the men would unearth sacred carvings and figurines that were stored under the house floors.

The third day was the Day of Feathers, when all participants wore feathered headbands and spent the day singing, while their guests cried out in the voices of their animal alter egos: seals, walruses, foxes, bears, ptarmigans, owls. That day too a wooden top decorated with feathers would be spun as a portent of the future. If it revolved freely and the eagle down stuck to its sides flew off, all would be well in the coming year.

On the final day, that of Calling, the singing reached a climax. Each boat-owner's name would be called in turn, and he would respond by crying out, "I want to take a whale! Right now!" Then the figurines would be produced; each in turn was used as the basis for a whaling story, at the end of which the hunters would prod it with spears to simulate a kill. The festivities came to an end on a lighter note, with everyone joining in a party for which they dressed up crazily, turning their clothing inside out or upside down – after which the communal houses would be shut for all but a few shamans' seances, to be reopened the next autumn in time for another ritual year.

Stories Told in String

To while away the long Arctic winters, Inuit still enjoy making intricate string figures that often tell a story or articulate a moral.

As in the game of cat's cradle, the figures are shaped from a single loop of string which can be manipulated into a seemingly endless number of designs. Favourite subjects are animals, often shown in a stylized way; so a fox would be represented by its bushy tail or a caribou by its antlers. Sometimes the makers – typically women, children or old people – weave several patterns in sequence to illustrate a simple story: the tale of a lemming falling through a smoke-hole, maybe, or of how a ptarmigan became snared in a thicket.

Like almost every other aspect of Inuit life, this seemingly simple pastime also sometimes takes on a wider mythical significance. In many parts of Canada and Alaska it is commonly played in autumn, supposedly so the declining sun may be caught in the meshes of the string and so be prevented from going away. Conversely, people sometimes cut the string loops to pieces when the sun is due to reappear at the end of winter to avoid any risk of entanglement, and will only take up the hobby again once its orb has safely emerged above the horizon.

111

Festivals of Giving

The traditional Arctic way of life insisted that much was shared, ensuring that everyone remained on fairly equal economic terms. When the fur trade made some Alaskan Indian peoples rich, however, it led to ritual displays of generosity known as potlatches.

While the Yupik and Inupiat lived with the constant threat of famine, things were very different in the forested lands to the south. The peoples who inhabited the northwest Pacific coast were fortunate in having the resources of the forests, the sea and of salmon-rich rivers. Although they too occasionally knew hard times, they mostly enjoyed lives of relative plenty. And for a brief time after the coming of Russian and Canadian fur traders, subsistence blossomed into genuine affluence.

Yet prosperity created a real dilemma for a society emphasizing co-operation and sharing. The tribes were hierarchical in structure, with powerful chiefs and elaborate gradations of rank. But the hierarchy was one of kin, for with the exception of an underclass of slaves, everyone in the community was more or less closely related. To accumulate excessive individual riches in such an environment was to cut oneself off from the goodwill and respect of one's own people.

The solution lay in potlatches, feasts accompanied by lavish gift-giving. Not only did the potlatch allow surplus wealth to be redistributed around the tribe and its neighbours; it also reinforced the status of the host by allowing him to display both his prosperity and his generosity.

The potlatch ceremony was developed to its greatest extent among such peoples of the Canadian coast as the Haida and the Kwakiutl, whose chiefs often gave away staggering amounts of wealth in the form of food, vessels, copper plates, masks, blankets and other goods. While not quite on the same scale, those of other Indians further north in Alaska were still considerable. For the northwest coast peoples, the occasion for a potlatch was usually the raising of a communal greathouse or the accession of a new chief. Among the Alaskans, for whom the events were altogether less elaborate affairs, they served to mark births and deaths or as marriage feasts, their scope and size reflecting the status of the husband. They were highly ritualized, complete with speeches of welcome, dances and specially composed songs.

One example, performed by a woman at a gathering at Carcross in the Yukon in 1912, was a variation on a familiar theme, the worm that keeps on growing. This story, however, is given a twist in the sympathy shown for the creature.

It tells how two young men find a worm while cutting wood. It seems frozen stiff, so they give it to a girl cousin who happens to be nearby. As they do so, one of the boys says teasingly, "We found a son for you".

The girl takes the worm home and thaws it out. It turns out not to be dead after all, so she decides to adopt it. At first she feeds it cooking fat, but as it grows bigger she takes to suckling it at her breast. In time she grows so attached to it that she rarely leaves her room, spending whole days nursing it and crooning to it.

Her parents become worried by her seclusion, and are horrified to discover its cause. So they invent a ruse to get the girl out of the house and kill the worm.

Hearing a commotion, she rushes back, too late to save the creature that has become her surrogate child. When she sees the worm dead, she is inconsolable, crying out between her sobs that she has lost a son, and she insists that her family compensate by cremating it, as though it had been a human being. "That's why they wrapped it in a button blanket and burned it," the song concludes. "That's the time she first sang this song. She made this song up while the worm was burning."

The Porcupine-Eater

The necessity of sharing essentials meant that generosity was an important virtue for the people of Alaska. This made greed a punishable vice – as one selfish husband discovered to his cost.

A man with two wives grew tired of sharing the game that he trapped with his partners, and started eating some of the best parts himself before he brought home the day's kill.

In particular he had a fondness for the layer of fat that keeps female porcupines warm in the long winter. But he did not realize that his wife had shamanic power that enabled her to know exactly what he got up to on his own in the forest. And it just so happened that her animal spirit helper was a porcupine.

The result was that the next time he settled down to a tasty snack, his wife used her magical abilities to make the dead porcupine's jaws fasten onto his lips, preventing him from eating anything. However hard he tried, he could not get the creature off. His wife only relented and made it let go after he had promised never again to indulge himself so selfishly.

The Magical Allure of Music

The tales told by Arctic peoples could summon stirring images in the minds of listeners. Music, however, had a still greater power, for singing was a religious act, and the shaman's drum a magic vehicle that could transport the singer to the world of spirits.

Throughout the entire Arctic region, music was everywhere – and it was usually accomplished with just the hand-drum and the human voice, which often had a distinctive, nasal intonation. People sang at work and at play. They crooned lullabies to babies. They performed in public, while feasting or dancing. And they used songs and rhythms to enter shamanic trances and contact the world of the spirits.

Some of the songs they sang were traditional, dealing with such themes as love, warfare, blood-feuds and, of course, hunting. But many were the singer's own, either composed for special events or else improvised from experience. Asked by a Danish anthropologist how many songs he had written, one Alaskan replied, "I only know I have composed many. Everything in me is song. I sing as I draw breath".

One distinctive Inuit tradition was that of the lampoon song, poking fun at anyone who had contravened accepted codes of behaviour or behaved in a selfish or arrogant manner. Among the eastern Inuit there were formalized song duels, in which feuding parties would cast derisive epithets in one another's face at public gatherings. Usually these exercises were relatively light-hearted and served to defuse tensions. On occasions, however, they turned into confrontations that could end in blows or even knife-fights.

Songs could also be used to right wrongs. One Inuit tale tells of a rejected wife who took advantage of a winter festival to shame her unfaithful husband publicly. She sang of the deadly harm he had done to her and their children by deserting them, leaving them to suffer hunger and neglect. As she rehearsed her grievances, she placed a bowl on the floor and set it spinning.

Before long the whole communal house seemed to turn with it, accelerating until it flew off to the spirit world, taking the entire village with it.

A Feast of Fellow Flesh

A similar theme of public shaming through song plays a part in a dark tale of an Inuit Bluebeard recorded in Greenland in the nineteenth century, when starvation was still a real threat and the horrors of cannibalism haunted the popular imagination. The story told of a man called Igimarasugsuk, who was rumoured to have had and lost a surprising number of wives. But he was a fine hunter, and his marital misfortunes were merely put down to the rigours of life in the isolated hut where he dwelled. When, wifeless again, he approached an unmarried woman from a large family, she was happy enough to go and live with him, taking with her a younger brother to relieve the pressure on her parents' home.

One day, returning from hunting reindeer, Igimarasugsuk asked the young man to go and fetch his axe, then followed him outside. Suddenly screams rent the air. Looking out, the wife saw her husband pursuing her brother with the axe, and as she looked on in horror he cut him down and killed him. Worse was to follow, for he gave her parts of the body to cook, insisting that she join him in dining off her own brother's flesh.

Now the wife knew for sure that her husband was a cannibal, but she had no way of escaping from him over the icy wastes. From that time on he rarely let her out of the house and fed her exclusively on reindeer-tallow. The terrible truth dawned on her that he was fattening her up with a view to eating her too.

A shaman's drum and *tupilaq*, a symbolic figure designed to negotiate with spirits summoned by the rhythm, from Nelson Island, *c.*19th century. The holes in its hands represent gaps in the sky through which animal spirits pass to replenish life on Earth.

How Song Came to the Saami

According to a legend of the Saami people in Lapland, the gentle gift of music was provided to them by the kind-hearted daughter of the sun.

The Saami claim that the art of song came to Earth with Akanidi, the daughter of the sun, who on her daily journeys across the heavens noticed that the people below her seemed listless and sad. So she won her father's permission to visit them. She fetched up in the house of an old and childless couple who lived on a lake island. They treated her as their own daughter, but would only allow her out to mix with other people once she had come of age.

When she was old enough, she wandered off into the world and achieved great things. She introduced all the people she met to the joys of singing and dancing, and also taught them how to make the colourful costumes for which Laplanders have ever since been famous.

Yet not everyone was happy with her innovations. The elders of the tribe wanted nothing to do with the new ways. All that interested them were the gemstones she magically produced to adorn jackets and skirts – and then only so that they could exchange them for valuable trade goods.

When Akanidi, sensing their greed, refused to supply any more, they plotted to kill her. Knowing that she was protected by the sun, they sought the aid of an old witch named Oadz. Oadz suggested blocking the smoke-hole of Akanidi's tent so the sun could not see them battering her to death.

But the murderers in their haste failed to block the hole entirely. So, when they struck Akanidi down, she did not die. Instead she faded into translucence; then, singing a final song, she floated up like firesmoke and disappeared for ever from human sight.

Yet she still looks down on the world from the heavens. And every time she spots people singing, she smiles, for she knows that she did not make her journey in vain.

In desperation, she decided her only hope lay in flight. Off she ran but she was pursued, and her husband would have caught her, but in her time of trial she found she possessed shamanic powers whose existence she had never guessed. With their aid, she managed to reach the safety of the nearest neighbours' house.

She had hardly had time to explain her plight when her husband arrived after her, hot on her trail. Quickly the neighbours hid her behind a skin curtain, then greeted Igimarasugsuk with every appearance of civility, offering him food as tradition demanded.

When he had eaten, they suggested – again in accordance with custom – that their guest should sing to entertain them. He declined, asking his host for a song instead. At that, the neighbour seized his opportunity. Using the convention of lampooning, he sang of a wicked husband who had killed all his wives. Then, mentioning Igimarasugsuk by name, he accused him of the ultimate horror of cannibalism. Blushing, the hunter rose to his feet, but the others siezed him; and at that moment his wife emerged from behind the curtain with a lance and stabbed him to death, just as he had hoped to kill her back at their own homestead in order to eat her for his dinner.

Songs of the Shamans

The most powerful songs of all were those of the shamans, who sang to enter trances or to summon up spirits. The words often came to them on soul-flights, inspired directly, they said, by the spirits they had contacted. As they sang, they would accompany themselves on hand-drums, typically tambours made of sealskin stretched across a hoop of wood. The drum-beat and the shaman's words would call the spirits near.

This tradition was shared by the Siberian tribes. Sakha (Yakut) shamans sometimes called their drums "reindeer", regarding them as the mounts that carried them to the spirit realm. In other parts of the Arctic, the instruments were seen as "horses" or "canoes" for similar reasons.

Sometimes the drums were believed literally to have a life of their own. Southern Greenlanders told a tale of a famous shaman called Kuanak whose drum once took flight after he himself had gone off on a soul journey. It flew around the communal house of its own accord for some time, then suddenly dropped to the ground. At that very moment, Kuanak's voice was heard outside, calling for help. Running to his aid, the observers found the shaman lying half-dead in the snow. His trance had been rudely interrupted by the chance sight of an old kayak cover – an emblem of death, as the skins were often used to carry corpses – and the shock had broken his concentration, with almost fatal consequences.

Another story told by the people of the Tikigaq peninsula reflects the complex way in which, in western Alaska, music, shamanism and magic could come together with the perennial concern with whale-hunting. It tells of a man who went off on a hunt, leaving his wife behind to support him through ritual inactivity at home (see page 123). As she lay motionless, her father-in-law took advantage of her, using a shaman's song to hypnotize her while he raped her.

The wife knew nothing of what had happened, and neither would the husband have known. But when he returned home his drum, which had been hanging on the wall throughout, sang out of its own accord, repeating the lascivious words of the seducer's song. Stricken with guilt and fear, the father-in-law snatched it angrily down and hurled it into the dwelling's entrance-passage, where it vanished without trace. Later that day, the hunter took his own life, unable to come to terms with what had happened.

Some time later, a dead whale drifted up to the village. Cutting up their chance catch, hunters found a drum caught in its gullet. The widow quickly recognized it as her husband's. In the shaman's world of shape-shifting and transformations, house and whale had somehow become one, and the magical drum thrown into the entrance-passage had ended up fatally lodged in the whale's air-passage.

117

The Significance of a Name

For the Inuit, individuals were made up of their physical presence, their souls and their names. Calling a new-born baby after a dead person guaranteed the deceased a kind of reincarnation, and meant the child would share some characteristics of its late namesake.

Across much of the northern world, names had a life of their own. There was a power in them that passed down through all those that bore them. When the individual who currently incarnated a name died, it remained homeless, and so a source of fear and taboo, until rehoused in a new-born infant. The act of bestowing it had considerable significance for the child, for along with the name itself, he or she could expect to acquire some aspects of the dead person's personality.

In the belief in the continuity of names there were elements of a theory of reincarnation. Yet in Inuit societies these were generally not applied rigorously. There were no Dalai Lama-like searches to find a dead person's spiritual heir. Instead the name would tradition-ally be given to the next child to be born into the community – an act of random selection made possible because the same names were used for boys and girls alike. Similarly, more than one baby could be named after someone who had recently passed away. At most, however, dreams would be analyzed and the physical appearance of the new-born scrutinized for signs of resem-blance. In parts of Asia where

Carving from Greenland of a woman carrying a baby in her sealskin parka. The first symbol of security for a child was giving it an auspicious name or one belonging to a trusted forebear.

the sense of lineage was strong, people's names would be passed down only among their own direct descendants, as among the Evenk.

The significance accorded to names produced some interesting results. For example, Inuit parents would sometimes address their baby as "mother" or "grandfather", since they could not bring them-selves to speak disrespectfully to the dead people whose names the youngsters bore. The custom could also help to explain sickliness in a child, which was often blamed on a mismatch with the name he or she had been given. In such cases the infant was sometimes renamed in the hope of bringing about a cure.

There were implications, too, for unnamed babies. In the rare cases when the threat of immi-nent starvation led to infanticide, the victims were always killed before they had been named, being regarded as still not fully human up to that time.

Names Without Bodies

Concerns over the homeless names of the recently dead also had an effect on behaviour. Some groups believed that merely uttering these could cause the deceased, caught in a limbo between life and death, to haunt the unwary speaker. The prob-lem was particularly acute when the name in ques-tion happened also to be that of some common household possession, in which case everyone would have to use cumbersome circumlocutions whenever they wanted to refer to it.

Another consequence was that a bond existed between people bearing the same name, even if they came from different communities and were not linked in any other way. In some regions, namesakes would give each other presents or else meet up for group reunions, rather as people sharing surnames sometimes do in the USA today. The unspoken assumption was that namesakes had something in common, even if their physical appearance and background were very different.

A new-born child's relationship with a deceased namesake was still more complicated. Relatives of the dead person would give presents to the infant as they would have done to their own loved one. The relationship was seen as parallel, for gifts given to the youngster by its parents were thought to be shared by the previous owner of the name in the afterlife.

A story told in the Yupik community about a girl who came back from the dead made this very clear. It recounted how a girl died, passing over into the afterlife. Not long afterwards a new baby girl was born in her village and was given her name. From that time on, whenever the new-born received a significant gift like a parka, the dead girl would attend the gift-giving, journeying back to the world of the living to be invisibly present.

There were strict rules governing travel between the two worlds, however, and she broke one of them. Instructed to climb over a fallen tree barring her path, she tripped and so broke the taboo. She lost consciousness at that point, and woke up again back in the living world in her old village.

When she was discovered, there was amazement, for no one had ever been seen to come back from the land of the dead. The surprise only increased when it was realized that she was wearing several parkas, one on top of the other. Not merely were they identical to the ones that had been given to her namesake; there were also the same number that the young child had received.

But for the parents of the new-born, the return brought only grief. With her namesake back in the land of the living, their own child sickened and died. The name wanted only one owner, and the dead girl had reclaimed her own.

In addition to the important naming ritual, clothing such as this girl's caribou-skin parka from West Greenland, was also offered to new-born infants. The ceremony was of such significance that the dead would travel back to the land of the living for the parka-giving ceremony of the baby who bore their name.

Focusing Female Power

In the Inuit world, the roles of the sexes were strictly defined and complementary. Women had dangerous powers that needed to be tightly controlled if they were not to sow disorder and drive the game away.

One shaman's wife explained that there used to be a world before the present one, but the sky had fallen on it and swept it all away. After this catastrophe, she recounted, there was nothing but darkness, confusion and chaos. At last, however, a new creation began to emerge from a lowly hummock of earth. It gave birth to two men who issued from the ground fully formed as adults. But this only posed a further problem, for there was no future in a world populated exclusively by men. So one of them sang a magical shaman's song and immediately turned into a woman. Then man and woman came together and had children, and from their union all the lands were populated.

A Division of Roles

The Inuit had firm views on the respective roles of the sexes, which were strictly enforced by an intricate web of taboos. The fundamental division was that men were responsible for all hunting of large game, while women had charge of processing the catch and preparing it as food. Other tasks that fell within the male domain include boat- and house-building, making tools and weapons and, if necessary, fighting off any threat to the community.

Women reared the children and looked after the day-to-day running of the household. They prepared skins (though flensing might also be done by the men) and made clothes and footwear. They fetched ice to melt for water, and were also for the most part responsible for the gathering aspects of the hunter-gatherer lifestyle, combing the neighbourhood of settlements in search of leaves, berries, grasses and roots. In some communities they might also trap small animals and certain kinds of birds and fish.

This time-honoured division of labour was rarely questioned, and there was strong disapproval of anyone who tried to upset the traditional order. A whole group of stories spelled out the miserable fate awaiting those who chose not to conform. A typical example from Greenland described how a widow named Arnarkuak, who lived with her son and daughter-in-law, spent all her time criticizing the young man for not having

more success in the hunt. Eventually her patience cracked altogether. Waiting until he had gone out in his kayak one day, she persuaded his wife to run away with her into the interior of the country. There the couple lived as man and wife, fending for themselves in the wilderness. But, the story concluded, the outraged husband tracked them down and ruthlessly killed his most unnatural mother.

A Woman's Revenge

Retribution could also await male sexual transgressors, as a tale from the Tikigaq peninsula in northern Alaska, spelled out. It told of a woman who refused to take a husband, and of the resentment this caused among the many single men of her community. Eventually, to punish her, she was dragged into the men's house and violated. The most violent of her attackers was a man called Aaliaq.

The woman's own father watched through the skylight of the house, powerless to intervene. But when the brutal attack was over, he shouted to her to wipe up the blood she had lost with the hem of her own parka.

An Inuit bag made from seal gut and feathers produced by skilled seamstresses. The waterproof clothing and containers were indispensable under Arctic conditions. Such items were also a major source of female status.

Back home, he cut out the blood-stained patch from her coat and used the material to fashion a tiny whale. He took this to a pool a short distance from the village and slipped it into the water. Then he sang a shaman's song, calling down vengeance on his daughter's ravishers in general and on Aaliaq in particular.

As he sang, the tiny toy figure came to life. It dived and rose again in the water just like a real whale. And then it began to grow. Before it grew too big, however, the man moved it to a larger pond, where it continued to swell up. Finally, he took it to the beach and lowered it into the open sea.

Soon it was the size of a full-grown bowhead. At that point the hunters in the village spotted it and hurried to their boats to set off in pursuit. Before long, most turned away, perhaps sensing that there was something strange about this particular quarry, leaving only Aaliaq to continue the chase. Closing on the great creature, he hurled his harpoon into its flank. But instead of seeking to escape by diving, it turned on Aaliaq and with one sweep of its tail smashed his delicate skinboat to smithereens. Great waves at once swamped the wreckage and Aaliaq was drowned. The girl and her father now had their revenge upon him.

As the story suggests, there was a particular awe of women's generative role, and a whole range of taboos and prohibitions aimed to keep these special powers in check. Menstruation was a particularly dangerous period. When a young girl first reached puberty, she had to avoid handling

This decorated yoke was used by women to carry heavy packs, part of the daily domestic burden. It was placed across the bearer's chest, lashing the load to the woman's back. A female face adorns the front and is inset with caribou teeth to protect the traveller from harm.

any kind of fresh food for several months and was expected to keep her eyes cast down to avoid looking anyone in the face. She was not allowed to travel in a boat or to break river ice lest the fish should be scared away.

At other times too female company could be dangerous for hunters. Even breathing in the air that women had exhaled could scare away animals, so hunters took care whenever possible to pass girls by on the windward side. Looking women in the eyes could damage a hunter's vision, so girls were encouraged never to look directly at them. One unstated side-effect of these prohibitions was to discourage sexual relations outside marriage. In a roundabout way this probably did encourage the energetic pursuit of game, since only successful hunters could afford to get married and so find sexual fulfillment.

The intensity of women's sexual power, and its relationship to the whales on which the community depended for food, gave women an important and subtle role in the business of the hunt. Among the northern Alaskan Inuit, wives shadowed every aspect of their husband's whaling

The Beneficial Power of Dreams

A dream could provide a window into the world of spirits and sometimes served as a premonition of things to come, having both a religious and practical significance.

For many northern peoples, dreams had a strong religious significance. Shamans looked to them as well as to trances to contact their spirit helpers and enter an alternative reality. "We believe that people can live a life apart from real life," a Netsilik Inuit told a researcher, "a life they can go through in their sleep."

Sometimes they could also come to people's aid in a more practical way. A Caribou Inuit story told of a woman in time of famine who dreamed that there were salmon trout in a nearby lake and saved her family from starvation when the fish were duly found and caught.

And in some Siberian communities, erotic dreams were said to portend success in the hunt – for the beautiful girl who visited the sleeping hunter was in fact none other than the spirit of the land.

The Inuit told a story that once a woman dreamed where to find salmon – and thereby saved her family from starvation.

adventures in an apparently passive way that was nonetheless considered vital to the success of the whole enterprise.

The wife's role started when the skinboat was first taken out to the shore each year, when she went on ahead. At the juncture with the sea-ice she halted and stayed behind while the boat was launched. Then she would lie down on the ice, her head pointing inland. The boat would circle and return to shore, where the harpooner would stretch out to touch her on the nape of the neck with his weapon. For an instant she personified the whale the men were seeking. Then she stood up and walked back to the village, leaving her belt and a mitten behind and taking care never to look back at the sea.

From then on her part was to do nothing. She was not permitted to comb her hair or pay any attention to her appearance. She could not sew or use a knife lest she cut the harpoon line anchoring the whale. She did not eat or sleep during her vigil, which in western Greenland was conducted indoors in darkness. Instead she entered a kind of trance, focusing all her mental energy on the hunt. The power of her concentration had to mirror that of the men in the boat; and if they met with success, the credit was as much hers as it was any of the other crew members'.

An Alaskan story brings home clearly the supernatural force that a hunter's wife of unusual spiritual power was thought able to generate. It tells of a woman called Suluk, the wife of a whale hunter named Kakianaq. Suluk went through the ritual on the ice as the boat was launched, and as she lay prone she heard a whale rise, summoned by her own shamanic powers.

Even though she could hear the frantic shouts as her husband's crew pursued their quarry, she did not let her concentration weaken. Instead she rose and headed back to the village, intoning a shaman's song. As she walked, a flock of ducks flew overhead. Without breaking her song, she raised one arm towards them, and a bird fell from the sky dead, killed by the strength of her magic.

While her husband was out hunting, Suluk managed to make his whale-float appear before her. This cap of a plug from a sealskin drag float served both a practical purpose (stopping the air from escaping) as well as a magical one: the carved female face, with traditional chin tattoo, acted as a charm to invoke successful hunting.

Then she returned home and sat quietly by the sleeping bench. Suddenly she heard noises coming from the iglu's entrance passage. Unmistakably it was the sound of the sea, but there was a particular note to it that at first she did not recognize. Then suddenly she knew it; it was the slapping sound a whale-float makes upon the swell after a kill. Going over, she found an actual float on the floor and, looking at it closely, realized from the markings on it that it was one of her husband's. She had caused it to materialize by thought alone; such was the magical power that could reside in a woman's concentration.

123

The Lore of Marriage

The extended family was the central element of Inuit society, and marriage was a vital step. Yet finding a suitable partner in the lonely northern wastes was not always easy – and in legends it was complicated by shape-shifting between animals and humans.

Given the often isolated nature of Inuit marriage, with the partners enjoying little company apart from that of each other and their close families, choosing husbands or wives was a decision that had to be made very carefully indeed. But parents traditionally expected to have a say in the match even when they did not arrange it, and prospective candidates would be weighed up carefully when they came to visit.

What the families were looking for, however, was not only physical attractiveness or social graces. According to one anthropologist who studied the Alaskan Yupik people, "the most important consideration in choosing a marriage partner was not the person's appearance, wealth, or social standing, but that person's careful, respectful and honest handling of food". Partners like the porcupine-eater (see page 113) who might stash away scarce delicacies to feast on in private, therefore, were particularly to be avoided.

Equally important was a sense of frugality. Some prospective parents-in-law applied an informal test, offering girls their son brought home a snack of crumbly dried fish. It was a good sign if they ate up all the crumbs, indicating a thrifty disposition; sweeping them onto the floor could suggest extravagance.

Marriage itself came in many different forms across the Inuit world. Often there was very little formality to the arrangement; a couple would simply start living together without any public announcement or ceremony. Elsewhere matches were pre-arranged by parents; the Caribou Inuit on the western shores of Hudson Bay, whose territories were sparsely populated even by Arctic standards, often set up future unions while the boy and girl were still infants.

The Aleut and some southwestern Alaskan groups had a well-established system of bride service in which the suitor lived with and worked for his future in-laws for some months before the match was consummated. There were even regions in which polygamy was practised, though only the very best hunters could contemplate the prospect of feeding more than one wife. Among the Aleut it was acceptable for a woman to have more than one husband, though again the doubling-up of work involved, this time for the wife, made the prospect uninviting.

Both polygamy and ·polyandry tended to occur in places where there was an extreme shortage of partners of the opposite sex. Through much of the Arctic world, the sheer scarcity of people severely restricted the choice and made incest a real danger. Some Inuit communities were forced by simple demography to turn a blind eye to marriages between cousins; in fact the Caribou Inuit even made a virtue of it.

Kala the Stony-Hearted

In a world where economic survival depended on the couple, one Inuit tale emphasized the necessity for all women to marry. It concerned an unmarried girl called Kala who had obstinately fallen into the habit of refusing all suitors.

One day, Kala was standing on a headland when two hunters in kayaks came paddling by. One called out to her that he had no wife. Would she not go with him? Unmoved, Kala did not deign to answer. She kept on gazing out to sea. The kayaks moved on. Suddenly Kala felt a stiffness in her limbs. Looking down, she saw with horror that her legs had turned to stone. Too late, she called

The Girl Who Married a Dog

In a world of shape-shifters, husbands were not always what they seemed to be – as one Inuit girl found out to the cost of herself and her family.

There was once a girl who would not take a husband. Angered by her stubbornness, her father one day shouted at her, "If there is no man good enough for you, why don't you marry a dog?"

The next day a new suitor came to their camp, and the girl noticed that he wore an amulet of dog-claws. This time her father would brook no refusal, so she agreed to go and live with the stranger on an island off the coast nearby. But she soon realized that her husband was actually a dog who could take on human form. Her suspicions were confirmed when, having become pregnant, she bore a litter of five human babies and five puppies.

Being a dog, her husband could not go hunting to provide for her and her offspring. Instead, he would swim across the sound to pick up packs of meat provided by the girl's father. But eventually the old man tired of the chore and put in boulders with the meat that so weighed down the dog that it sank and drowned.

Now the girl had no one to support her. Blaming her father for her predicament, she set her dog-children on him next time he paddled across to see her, and they mauled him so badly that he died. Left with ten hungry mouths to feed, and no easy way to gather food, she eventually decided that she would have to send her children out into the world to fend for themselves. So by magic she transformed her boots into boats and dispatched all ten – and they became the ancestors of both the native North American peoples and of white men.

out after the men, begging them to come back. But they paddled on. Next her torso grew rigid, then her neck and arms. Before long only her navel remained flesh as a reminder that she had ever been human. For the Stone Spirit had married Kala, as it does all those for whom human partners are just not good enough. And she remains on that lonely eminence to this day, petrified by the hardness of her own heart.

Crossing Boundaries

Arctic myth regarded the boundaries between the human and animal worlds as fluid and a whole genre of folktales grew up in which humans took animal partners. And yet there was an unease about crossing the divide and the stories almost always ended unhappily. The girl who married an eagle went mad and died after giving birth to a baby that was half-bird and half-man; the man whose wife was a vixen killed himself when she ran away back to the wild; the woman abducted by a whale was kept tied by a rope to the seabed and had to be rescued at great peril by her two brothers.

Although it shares an unhappy ending, one such narrative, collected in the mid-nineteenth century, bears interesting parallels with the theme of the love of a man for a bird-woman familiar from folktales around the world (not least from the ballet *Swan Lake*). In the Inuit version, though, the protagonist is no romantic hero but an old bachelor – a stock figure of fun in Arctic stories.

One day, it recounts, the man happened by chance on a lake in which many women were bathing. Sensing an opportunity, he sneaked over to the place where they had left their clothes. Catching sight of him, they all rushed to cover their nakedness and then took flight in the most literal sense, for as soon as they put on their clothes they turned into birds. But he held back the garb of the prettiest, who thus remained grounded. When he asked her to be his wife, she had little alternative but to accept the offer.

The couple returned to the hunter's home and set up house together. At first the husband refused to leave the iglu even to go hunting, fearing that he would come back to find his treasured wife gone. But eventually his confidence in her increased to the point when he happily left her all day long.

In time his wife bore him two strapping sons, and he considered her fully reconciled to the human world. But in fact she still had dreams of escape. When the boys were old enough to roam outside the village, she encouraged them to search for bird feathers, and before long they had gathered enough for her to make three sets of wings – two for the children and one for herself. Donning them, all three immediately turned into seagulls and flew away.

Returning home, the old man was desolate to find himself alone in the world once more, and he set off at once to try to find his lost family. For many weeks he wandered back and forth across the land, but in vain. Eventually, however, he met a shaman who told him how to track the fugitives down. With this secret knowledge he finally found them – they were living in human guise in a house that seemed at first sight to be much like the one they had left, though they evidently shared this one with many other occupants. Looking in through a window, he saw his wife in conversation with a man with a prominent, beak-like nose. He could hear that the stranger was pestering her to marry him but she was refusing the offer.

The old man waited for what seemed like hours. One by one the other occupants left the house, until eventually only his wife and the

Carved wooden bowl in the form of a bird, from Kodiak Island, Alaska. Although many Arctic tribes believed in the communality of human and animal souls, stories often warned against marriages between the two.

stranger were left. When he too finally came out-side, the husband thought his chance had come and he slipped inside to reclaim the bride he desired. But it was not to be. Seeing him coming, she rushed for the open door and soared heaven-wards, a gull once more. Her beak-nosed suitor followed her, transformed into a wild duck. And when the hunter turned back towards the house, he found it too had gone: it had changed into a gull-hill and was now nothing more than a ragged mound of turf and moss of the kind that gulls choose to make their nests in.

Home-sickness for one's own world is a recurrent theme in Inuit tales of marriages between humans and non-humans. It informs one of the best-known of all their legends: the story of the star husbands and their human brides (see page 38). In one variant, the women discover that not only stars but animals as well are unsuitable part-ners, however desperate they may be.

When the women successfully escaped from their new home in the heavens it seemed their troubles were over at last – but they landed on top of a large tree and could find no way of getting down. They waited for what seemed like an eter-nity, increasingly anxious that their efforts to return home had been confounded. But eventually they spotted a wolverine and persuaded it to climb up the trunk to rescue them by deceitfully offering to marry it. They had learned their lesson, however, and as soon as they found themselves close to their parents' encampment they reneged on their promise and scampered home, resolved in future to limit their attentions to human suitors.

Two Inuit girls looked into the sky for their inspiration one evening and ended up with stars as their husbands. Moonglow on a frozen landscape in northern Greenland evokes memories of the two, who learned a valuable lesson.

Journey to the Land of the Dead

The Inuit believed that people were not single but multiple beings. They divided the self into more than simply body and soul, and thought that widely different fates awaited the various aspects of their identity after they ceased to exist.

In the Inuit view, a person was more than just a physical presence, or even a body and soul; other ingredients in the mix included a name, disposition and breath, which had a life of its own. Sometimes mind, voice and vision too were regarded as separate entities. Attitudes towards death were complicated by the need to explain the fate of each of these different components.

There was no argument about what would happen to the body, which simply decayed. Usually dead people were buried in shallow graves or, if the permafrost made digging impossible, were left on the ice and covered with rocks to keep off predators. The Aleut sometimes mummified their dead, while the Asian Eskimos ritually dismembered the bodies before burial.

Names were reincarnated in new-born babies, taking with them a part of the dead person's personality (see page 118). Breath simply ceased, as did mind, voice and vision. That left the soul, whose destiny was much more problematic.

The general view was that a person's soul left their body sometime shortly after death and went on a journey to the land of the dead. Although on a different level of existence to Earth, this was like the world they had left behind.

One of the clearest descriptions of this afterworld comes in the story of the girl who came back from the dead. It describes how she lost consciousness at death and came to again sometime afterwards to find herself travelling down a well-used trail, much like those she had known when she was alive. The path forked at various points, but each time she instinctively knew which was the right way for her to go. She reached her journey's end in a village not unlike the one she had lived in on Earth, where she was greeted by a recently deceased grandmother, who welcomed her into her home.

The path back to the world of the living remained open, and the couple would travel along it whenever there was a celebration for their namesakes. But the trip was a perilous one, and there was always a danger that a soul could get marooned. Such was the girl's fate when she contravened a taboo in the course of a return trip and woke up to find herself sprawled in the food cache of her native village. Fully alive once more, she survived to old age before once more passing the threshold to the land of the dead.

There were different traditions as to where the land or lands of the dead might lie. Many groups accepted the idea that there were two, one pleasant and the other unpleasant, but neatly inverted the view prevalent in most parts of the world as to where these were to be found. In an environment where snugness and comfort lay in burrowing down into the ground, the Inuit Heaven – a place of abundant game, where the dead person would meet friends and relatives who had

Funeral rituals among the Koryak involved the preparation of elaborate costumes for the dead. This man's funeral cap, from Siberia, is decorated with geometric patterning. Black was often associated with evil and death; white was neutral.

128

The House of Corpses

A story which describes the old days in Greenland captures the fear that the constant threat of unexpected death could generate in those living in isolated communities.

A shaman on Qeqertarsuaq, an island opposite what is now the Thule airbase, set off one day on his sledge to visit his married sister. He had almost reached her house when his dogs suddenly stopped, refusing to go any closer. Approaching the apparently deserted building on foot, he looked in through the window and saw to his horror the entire family frozen in death.

Only one occupant showed any sign of life, and that was his sister. When she saw him, she gave no sign of recognition but crept towards him, her mouth opening and closing hungrily. He fled in terror back to his sledge, but the dogs still refused to budge. Only when the spectre was quite close, jaws agape to devour man or dogs, did they suddenly jerk into action, not stopping again until they reached the safety of home.

Subsequently the shaman went on a soul-flight to find out the cause of the tragedy. He reported on his return that the entire household had been frightened to death by a premonitory apparition: the vision of a discarded kayak-skin used to carry a corpse to its final resting-place.

gone before – lay below the earth. Their equivalent of Hell, offering only starvation and cold, was situated up in the sky.

For those who survived, it was crucial to prepare the dead person suitably for their journey. The body was dressed warmly before burial in boots, mittens and a favourite parka, and food was prepared to sustain the spirit on its way. With typical thrift in an environment where scarcity was never far away, this was later consumed by the mourners in a meal which was also an act of communion with the dead. Favourite possessions were placed in or around the grave so that the deceased would have use of them in the afterlife.

It was equally important to set the spirit on the right path. Returning from the burial, the mourners would symbolically cut the path back to the village with a knife, or scatter ashes along the way, to stop the dead person from following them. But they avoided cutting the route to the land of the dead altogether, and for five days following the death the family would not use tools of any kind. A whole range of taboos affected the immediate family for as much as a year after the event; for above all the deceased person required respect and consideration if he or she was to remain contentedly on the right side of the boundary separating the quick from the dead.

129

A RICH HERITAGE RENEWED

In the twentieth century, Arctic peoples found themselves alienated from the rhythms of their traditional lifestyle and divorced from what the Inuit call the *nunatsiaq*, or "beautiful land", that had informed their culture for millennia. The stories that had captured the communities' essential truths had begun to lose their meaning; spiritual bonds had been lost. The decades following World War II, however, saw a reawakening of Inuit cultural consciousness reflected in the work of artists who began to reclaim ancient symbols and myths, and reinterpreted subjects, such as shamanism or the rituals of the hunt, that were in danger of becoming lost for ever under the more pressing social and political concerns of the younger generation.

Above: Grey stone figure entitled *Animal* by Andy Miki (1918–1983), from Whale Cove, Nunavut, 1967. As well as depicting the spirit of an animal, which may be a caribou, the sculpture recalls the ancient tradition of utility, for it fits comfortably into the hand like a stone tool.

Right: Embroidered felt piece called *Mysterious Powers of the Shaman* by Irene Avaalaaqiaq Tiktaalaaq, from Baker Lake, 1974. The influence of Communism in Siberia and of Christianity in the rest of the Arctic meant that shamanism became taboo throughout the region. It remained, however, central to the spiritual life of the people and is now re-emerging in many communities. This design was inspired by stories told by the artist's grandmother. The strange heads and beings conjured up by the shaman emphasize the interconnected nature of the spirit and animal worlds.

Left: Green stone figure of a spirit by Qavaroak Tunnillie. In earlier times the unpredictable nature of many spirits meant few people dared make physical representations of them. Today, however, malign forces are a popular subject for artists who are as likely to find forms in their own imagination as in ancient legend.

Below: Sculpture called *Dancing Bear*, by the Cape Dorset artist Pauta Saila, 1973. It is said that Arctic peoples learned how to hunt by watching polar bears which, with their ability to sit or stand to rest or look around, many Inuit felt to behave very like humans. Saila is best known for his humorous bear pieces.

Above: Mythology continues to inform modern Inuit art. This piece, by the Iglulik artist Yvonne Kayotak, from Nunavut, northeast Canada, represents Sedna, the Sea Mother. She is shown commanding the creatures of the sea – fish, seals and the narwhal – for it was at her behest that they gave themselves to hunters.

Right: The traditional woman's role in preparing the slaughtered animal is celebrated in this coloured woodcut by Bernard Tuglamena, from Katexac, King Island, 1963. The decline of hunting and its attendant ritual has been one of the major disruptions in Arctic culture. International law has played a part, but so too has technology – for as an old Caribou Eskimo once observed: with guns to make hunting easy, people became less conscientious about observing taboos.

Above: A Shaman's Helping Spirits by Jessie Oonark (1906–1985), from Baker Lake, stonecut and stencil, 1971. This shaman, wearing musk ox horns to attract his spirit helpers, literally embodies the physical and spiritual world of the Arctic. Shamans still remain powerful as images, symbolizing a world-view at odds with both modern society and the Christian missions. For a long time it seemed that the roles the shaman once provided for Arctic communities would be supplanted by the law, medicine and the Church. But many people today are trying to combine these with the spiritual heritage of their ancestors.

THE LEGACY OF ARCTIC MYTH

The first half of the twentieth century saw the peoples of the far north increasingly distanced from their cultural roots. The ancient stories and traditions through which their identities were expressed, however, survived the social pressures exerted by foreign influences and have made a dramatic return to the forefront of contemporary Arctic life.

The celebrated 1922 film *Nanook of the North*, by American explorer Robert Flaherty, projected the Inuit as a heroic savage – and for much of the twentieth century, Arctic peoples have laboured under outsiders' perceptions of them either as Flaherty's noble primitives or as "social problems" dependent on welfare handouts.

This image of the Inuit as a happy and heroic throwback to a long-lost age survived until the early 1950s. Then two Canadian books published in 1952 – *People of the Deer* by Farley Mowat and Richard Harrington's *The Face of the Arctic* – both drew attention to the conditions of severe hardship under which the Inuit lived, many close to starvation. Mowat's attack on the treatment of the Inuit by the Canadian government provoked a storm of public controversy and was angrily denounced as ill-informed by officials.

In the late 1950s and 1960s, however, the Canadian government acknowledged the problem and set out to tackle it by imposing a new way of life on the Inuit. Already in the 1940s northern Canada had been divided into twelve Eskimo Registration Districts, and individual Inuit had been given numbers that they were required to wear on a tag around their necks. Now some Canadian Inuit groups were forcibly relocated into permanent settlements; there were reports of hunters having their dogs rounded up and shot by the Royal Canadian Mounted Police. In some areas Inuit were required to try new ways of living such as herding yak and sheep or farming eiderduck.

It was a pattern repeated with other Arctic peoples at different times in the century. Settlement in villages and survival on welfare benefits or public-sector wages wrenched the native population from their familiar patterns of life and the intense relationship with the land that had once given them their identity. It also fostered hostility to traditional Arctic cultures.

In some places children were deposited in boarding schools and taught in a foreign language. Christian missionaries in North America and the Communist authorities in the then Soviet Union also tried to stamp out shamanic practices. In the USSR, shamans, renowned for their capacity to make soul-flights while in a trance (see page 86), were reportedly taken aloft in helicopters and challenged to prove their ability.

UNITED ARTISTS Present

"NANOOK OF THE NORTH"

Produced by ROBERT J. FLAHERTY

Publicity poster for Robert Flaherty's 1922 film, *Nanook of the North* which played up the Eskimo's primitive culture. At one point during filming, however, its star fixed Flaherty's camera.

A Cultural Revival

But over time, the Arctic peoples fought back. Coming together in their own political and cultural groupings, they opened the door to the past and also to a better future. In 1956 the Saami of northern Scandinavia and Russia launched the Nordic Saami Council, and in 1977 the Inuit Circumpolar Conference was established as a political forum for Inuit peoples. Inuit delegates from Greenland, the United States, Canada and Russia attended the final Circumpolar Conference of the century in Nuuk, Greenland, in late July 1998.

Underscoring these political achievements, however, has been the revival of indigenous cultural forms and the adaptation of wider cultural influences to an Arctic perspective.

Tukaq Theatre of Greenland was one of many theatrical groups which used folklore and traditional culture to explore contemporary issues. Tukaq, whose name means "Harpoon Head", was established in the mid-1970s and became the first

In the Soviet period many traditions of ritual song, dance and story-telling were permitted only in the controlled environment of schools and village halls. Here Nenets schoolgirls from Yamal, Siberia, perform a dance with ribbons which represent the sun.

professional theatre troupe in Greenland. Its first presentation was *Oqautsip Kimia* ("Power of the Word"). It followed this with the widely successful *Inuit*, which toured throughout the Arctic.

The latter play, set in a mythical past, told how a fearsome *tornaq* spirit wearing a symbolic white mask disrupted the harmonious existence of the Inuit and made them don masks and European-style clothing. The Inuit protagonists, feeling that they were losing their souls, called on the venerable spirits of their land for help. Aided by Inunerup Arna – "Woman of Life", a form of the Sea Mother (see page 58) – they were eventually able to regain their freedom. In the end the *tornaq* came to live in harmony with the Inuit who had finally vanquished it.

Arctic-born writers also made a telling contribution in novels and other prose writings. Perhaps the most celebrated of them was Markoosie, the first Canadian Inuit to publish a book in English when he released his novel *Harpoon of the Hunter* (1970) which was also published in Inuktitut. The year before her death in 1982, native Alaskan writer and educator Emily Ivanoff Brown Ticasuk published her retelling of a native Alaskan legend about a shaman in *The Longest Story Ever Told: Qayaq, the Magical Man*.

The trend is evident across the Arctic. The Saami Nils-Aslak Valkeapaa has won an international reputation as an artist, poet and musician. He is a celebrated performer of *joik*, traditional Saami folk-chants. Many Siberians have also been writing in Russian and in their native language.

Young Saami in their traditional finery, at the Easter reindeer races, Kautokeino, Norway. Many Saami were once ashamed of their identities but now they wear their costumes with pride.

The Greenlandic actors of Tukaq aimed to forge an Inuit acting style developed from drum dancing and story-telling meetings. Traditional songs used in the play were taken from those collected by the Danish-Inuit traveller Knud Rasmussen in the 1920s and 1930s. The Tukaq Theater successfully toured Canada and the United States, making it an inspirational beacon for other theatre groups in the Arctic region. It also played a major role in the creation of the Indigenous Peoples' Theatre Association, which was established in Toronto in 1980.

Much of their work aimed to reclaim elements once central to Inuit culture. In the 1980s the Alaskan Inuit Chevak Theater, produced a three-hour drama based on the traditional Bladder Festival, which celebrated the cyclical return of animal and human souls (see page 109). In the drama a "Westernized" Alaskan – materially wealthy but spiritually defunct, reduced to alcohol and despair – was restored to vitality through the traditional ceremonial of the festival.

The Struggle for a Homeland

In some areas, however, the desire of Arctic communities to revive their culture has met with resistance. Their traditions of marine hunting have brought them into conflict with Western environmentalists and regulatory bodies. Arctic peoples, however, found it arrogant when southern environmentalists, who shop in supermarkets and boutiques for products whose manufacture pollutes the Arctic with mercury, presumed to lecture them about the environment. They denounced the animal rights campaigners who have never had to depend on hunting to stay alive and whose activities reduced many native communities to destitution. One significant achievement has been to restore their birthright to subsistence whaling in the north Pacific, banned in the 1970s by the International Whaling Commission. This has been progressively restored through a painstaking procedure in which Inuit and Chukchi communities in Alaska and Siberia have been forced to take on and educate scientists and environmentalists.

Throughout the Arctic, there has also been growing pressure for ever-increasing levels of local self-government. In the 1950s, Greenland attained home rule while remaining under the Danish crown. In Alaska and Canada during the 1970s, legislation such as the Alaska Native Claims Settlement Act created numerous native corporations under which native communities managed their own land and invested their revenue.

The most recent achievement has been in northeastern Canada where, on 1 April 1999, the Inuit homeland of Nunavut ("Our Land" in the Inuktitut language) was inaugurated – the culmination of negotiations between Arctic Inuit and the Canadian government which began in the 1970s.

Under the new agreement, the eastern half of the former Northwest Territories becomes the new Inuit-governed Canadian homeland of Nunavut. The new territory covers an area of 1.9 million square kilometres – roughly the size of western Europe – and has a population of just 25,000, of whom 85 per cent are Inuit. It stretches from the border with Saskatchewan and Manitoba to Ellesmere and Baffin Islands. The agreement gives the Inuit legal title to around 350,000 square kilometres of land in Nunavut and mineral rights to around 35,000 square kilometres. Government is by a nineteen-member legislative assembly.

The new government has plans to promote Inuit culture and language in Nunavut. Inuktitut will be the primary language of government and schools, and pupils will be instructed in Inuit traditions. The Nunavut Wildlife Management Board has been established to enlarge official quotas for hunting polar bears, whales and seals.

Fireworks lit the sky over the territory's capital Iqaluit as Nunavut was born in the first minutes of 1 April. Celebrations included songs and drum dances and a feast of seal, musk ox and caribou. During the traumatic years of the Arctic's religious, economic and political colonization, the region's culture was ignored or denigrated by the colonizers. But at the end of the twentieth century – as the Canadian Inuit resume control of their political and cultural destiny, and other indigenous groups including the Saami assert themselves in diverse ways – this heritage in folklore, religion and musical forms is proving a rich source of inspiration.

It is likely that many more demands for self-government will be made around the Arctic. Indigenous people will continue to revive and preserve what they see as the best of their cultural heritage – a privilege taken for granted by most of the millions of people to the south.

The new era in the life of the indigenous peoples of the Arctic is shown at the inauguration ceremony for Nunavut where traditional costumes mix with a modern government institution.

Glossary

ajagak A hand-held game in which a piece of seal-bone has to be caught in the skin thong it is attached to.

angakoq The Inuit word for a shaman, the community's visionary who travelled to the spirit world to negotiate good hunting or the end of misfortunes.

angakua Iglulik Inuit word for the brilliant inner light that was the essential driving force of a shaman.

inua The "in-dwelling being" of an animal or person – its soul, which was not dependent on its body for existence.

inugluk Mask placed by whale-hunters of the Tikigak peninsula on sealskin floats which were attached to their harpoons. When a struck whale dived the mask sang back to the whalers, telling them the direction their injured prey would take as it tried to escape.

kele Spirit who brought harm to the Chukchi of northeast Siberia, often in the form of a disease or bad hunting.

kiviaq Raw auk meat, wrapped in parcels then fermented. A delicacy among the Kalaallit of Greenland.

kujjai Among the Even of Siberia, a consecrated reindeer which protects its owner from harm, and on which the owner's soul may ride to the sky to receive a blessing from the sun.

mitaartut Means, literally, "people in disguise", a word which gives itself to the Greenlandic festival of masks which is reminiscent of the more southerly, Western tradition of Halloween.

okamak A charm necklace, hung with amulets, and worn by the Chukchi people of Siberia to protect themselves from the influence of evil spirits.

qaculluut The name of the many-toothed wolf-fish of the Yupik people.

qaumaneq "Lightning", another Inuktiut term for *angakua*, the special spiritual power which sets a shaman apart from ordinary members of the community.

qasgiq Men's communal houses, which were the social and ceremonial centre of Inuit village life.

qivittut The mythic wild men who spurned the company of humans after tragedies – such as disappointment in love – and who then roamed the lands alone, living with the animals.

tupilaq Small effigy made by a shaman from animal skin and parts of human bodies and brought to life to track down and harm an enemy.

umiak Open boat built from driftwood and walrus-skin, used by the Inuit for whale-hunting. Such boats typically carried approximately eight people.

ulu Tool used by Inuit women to scrape blubber when preparing skins or hides.

yaranga A portable tent, usually constructed out of walrus hide, used by the nomadic Chukchi.

yua Another name for *inua*.

Index

Page numbers in *italic* denote captions. Where there is a textual reference to the topic on the same page as a caption, italics have not been used.

Further Reading

Birgsland and Dirks, *Aleut Tales and Narratives.* 1990.
Dolitsky, A.B. (ed.) *Fairy Tales and Myths of the Bering Strait Chukchi.* Alaska-Siberian Research Center, 1996.
Fienup-Riordan, A. *The Living Tradition of Yup'ik Masks.* University of Washington Press, Seattle, 1996.
Laguna, F. de (ed.) *Tales from the Dena.* University of Washington Press, Seattle, 1995.
Lopez, B. *Arctic Dreams.* Harvill, London, 1986.
Lowenstein, T. *Ancient Land: Sacred Whale.* Bloomsbury Publishing, London, 1993.
Norman, H. (ed.) *Northern Tales.* Pantheon Books, New York, 1990.
Nungak, Z. and E. Erima. *Inuit Stories.* Canadian Museum of Civilization, Quebec, 1988.
Nuttall, M. *Arctic Homeland.* Belhaven Press, London, 1992.
Rasmussen, K. *The Intellectual Culture of the Iglulik Eskimo.* Gyldendalske Boghandel, Copenhagen, 1929.
Riordan, J. *The Sun Maiden and the Crescent Moon.* Canongate, Edinburgh, 1989.
Vitebsky, P. *The Shaman.* Macmillan, London, 1995.

Picture Credits

Further Reading

Birgsland and Dirks, *Aleut Tales and Narratives*. 1990.
Dolitsky, A.B. (ed.) *Fairy Tales and Myths of the Bering Strait Chukchi*. Alaska-Siberian Research Center, 1996.
Fienup-Riordan, A. *The Living Tradition of Yup'ik Masks*. University of Washington Press, Seattle, 1996.
Laguna, F. de (ed.) *Tales from the Dena*. University of Washington Press, Seattle, 1995.
Lopez, B. *Arctic Dreams*. Harvill, London, 1986.
Lowenstein, T. *Ancient Land: Sacred Whale*. Bloomsbury Publishing, London, 1993.
Norman, H. (ed.) *Northern Tales*. Pantheon Books, New York, 1990.
Nungak, Z. and E. Erima. *Inuit Stories*. Canadian Museum of Civilization, Quebec, 1988.
Nuttall, M. *Arctic Homeland*. Belhaven Press, London, 1992.
Rasmussen, K. *The Intellectual Culture of the Iglulik Eskimo*. Gyldendalske Boghandel, Copenhagen, 1929.
Riordan, J. *The Sun Maiden and the Crescent Moon*. Canongate, Edinburgh, 1989.
Vitebsky, P. *The Shaman*. Macmillan, London, 1995.

Picture Credits

The publisher would like to thank the following people, museums and photographic libraries for permission to reproduce their material. Every care has been taken to trace copyright holders. However, if we have omitted anyone we apologize and will, if informed, make corrections in any future edition.

Key:
t top; **c** centre; **b** bottom; **l** left; **r** right

Abbreviations:

BM	British Museum, London
BCA	Bryan and Cherry Alexander
CAS	Center for Arctic Studies/Smithsonian Institution, Washington, DC
SJM	Sheldon Jackson Museum, Sitka, Alaska
WFA	Werner Forman Archive, London

Cover BCA; **cover surround** WFA; **title page** Alaska State Museum/Barry McWayne (II-A-5413); **contents page** BCA; **6** Christina Dodwell/Hutchison Picture Library; **7** WFA; **8** BCA; **9** WFA; **12** BCA; **13** University of Alaska Museum/WFA; **15t** Moravian Archives, Bethlem, Pennsylvania; **15c** SJM (II.H.46); **16** CAS (CXR AK 81); **17** CAS (AMNH 70-7689a, b); **18l** Canadian Museum of Civilisation (S91-919); **18r** WFA; **19** Canadian Museum of Civilisation/Jessie Oonark (S93-632); **20** The National Museum of Denmark, Department of Ethnography. Photographer Lennart Larsen; **21** WFA; **22c** BCA; **22cr** Smithsonian Institution/WFA; **22b** The Sainsbury Centre of Visual Arts, University of East Anglia; **23t** Smithsonian Institution/Salamander Books; **23b** Michael Holford; **24** BCA; **25** BCA; **26** Art Gallery of Ontario (T-1806-2); **27** University of Alaska Museum. Photographer Barry McWayne; **28–29** Smithsonian Institution, NMAI; **30** CAS (NMNH 176207); **31** WFA; **32** Alaska State Museum, Juneau. Photographer Barry McWayne; **34–35** Robert Harding Picture Library; **36** SJM (II.B.13); **37** Canadian Museum of Civilisation (S88-1190); **39** SJM (II.G.3, II.G.4, II.G.10); **40** Smithsonian Institution/WFA; **42** BM; **43** BCA; **44** Joe Cornish, Operation Raleigh International/Robert Harding Picture Library; **45** CAS (AMNH 70-2992); **46** CAS (AMNH 70-870a, b); **47** CAS (NMNH 375349); **48** CAS (AMNH 70-3655a, b); **50** Smithsonian Institution (SI 153624); **51** WFA; **52** Royal Geographical Society, London; **53** WFA; **54** WFA; **55** WFA; **56–57** NMAI (9/3574)57; **58** BCA; **59** WFA; **61** Dr Peter Furst; **62** BCA; **63** WFA; **64–65** Museum fur Volkerkunde, Berlin (IV6370); **68** University of Alaska Museum (UA314-4354); **69** WFA; **72t** The Greenland Museum/WFA; **72c** Alaska Gallery of Eskimo Art/WFA; **72b** Wolfgang Kaehler/Corbis; **73t** National Archives of Canada (PA53606); **73l** Peter Harholdt/Corbis; **73r** Smithsonian/MNAI; **74** CAS (Maritime Museum, Vladivostock 2180-8a); **75** BCA; **76** CAS (NMNH 56026); **78** Museum fur Volkerkunde, Berlin (IV4420); **79** Joe Cornish/Robert Harding Picture Library; **81** CAS (NMNH 393156); **82** Smithsonian/Salamander Books; **83** WFA; **84** BCA; **86** WFA; **87** WFA; **88** CAS (AMNH 70-7810); **89** WFA; **91** Robert H. Lowie Museum, University of California/WFA; **93** CAS (AMNH 337173, Jesup Expedition); **94** Manitoba Museum/WFA; **95** Staatlisches Museum fur Volkerkunde, Munich (Neg No. 12137); **96** BM/WFA; **97** William Channing Collection/WFA; **98t** BCA; **98b** Mystic Seaport Museum. Photographer George Comer (1966.339.11); **98–99** WFA; **99t** Staatlisches Museum fur Volkerkunde, Munich (Neg No. 11993); **99b** Smithsonian/NMAI (10.6091); **100** BCA; **101** WFA; **102** WFA; **103** BCA; **104** WFA; **105** WFA; **106** BCA; **106–107** BM; **108** BM; **109** WFA; **110** WFA; **115** SJM (II.S.171); **118** WFA; **119** BM; **120** WFA; **121** WFA; **123** Alaska Museum of Eskimo Art/WFA; **126** WFA; **127** BCA; **128** CAS (MAE 956-820); **130t** Andy Miki/Art Gallery of Ontario; **130–131t** Qavaroak Tunille, Cape Dorset/Art Gallery of Ontario (89/622); **130–131b** Irene Avaalaaqia/Canadian Museum of Civilisation; **131b** Pauta Saila, Cape Dorset/Art Gallery of Ontario (89/625); **132t** BCA; **132b** University of Alaska Museum/Barry McWayne; **133** Canadian Museum of Civilisations/Jessie Oonark (S90-1207); **134** Ronald Grant Archive; **135** BCA; **136** BCA; **137** BCA